MW00893631

Emeril Lagasse

French Door 360 Air Fryer

Cookbook for Beginners

Discover Effortless & Flavorful Cooking with 2000-Day Easy Emeril Lagasse
Recipes for Air Frying, Baking, and Roasting

Ariana Minch

© Copyright 2024 – All rights reserved

This document is geared towards providing exact and reliable information with regards to the topic and issue covered. The publication is sold with the idea that the publisher is not required to render accounting, officially permitted, or otherwise, qualified services. If advice is necessary, legal, or professional, a practiced individual in the profession should be ordered. -From a Declaration of Principles which was accepted and approved equally by a Committee of the American Bar Association and a Committee of Publishers and Associations. In no way is it legal to reproduce, duplicate, or transmit any part of this document in either electronic means or in printed format. Recording of this publication is strictly prohibited and any storage of this document is not allowed unless with written permission from the publisher.

All rights reserved. The information provided herein is stated to be truthful and consistent, in that any liability, in terms of inattention or otherwise, by any usage or abuse of any policies, processes, or directions contained within is the solitary and utter responsibility of the recipient reader.

Under no circumstances will any legal responsibility or blame be held against the publisher for any reparation, damages, or monetary loss due to the information herein, either directly or indirectly. Respective authors own all copyrights not held by the publisher.

The information herein is offered for informational purposes solely, and is universal as so. The presentation of the information is without contract or any type of guarantee assurance. The trademarks that are used are without any consent, and the publication of the trademark is without permission or backing by the trademark owner.

All trademarks and brands within this book are for clarifying purposes only and are the owned by the owners themselves, not affiliated with this document.

Table of Contents

Introduction

Welcome to the Emeril Lagasse French Door Air Fryer Oven Cookbook, your gateway to a world of culinary possibilities. This multifunctional appliance merges the ease of an air fryer with the capabilities of an oven, enabling you to effortlessly and accurately cook a variety of dishes. Whether you're a seasoned home cook or just beginning your culinary journey, this cookbook is your ultimate guide to mastering this innovative kitchen tool.

The Emeril Lagasse French Door Air Fryer Oven is more than just an air fryer—it's a multifunctional powerhouse that can bake, roast, toast, and dehydrate, all while delivering the crispy, golden results you expect from an air fryer. With its elegant French door design, this appliance not only looks stunning on your countertop but also offers a user-friendly experience, making it easy to access and monitor your food as it cooks.

In this cookbook, you'll find a carefully curated collection of recipes that showcase the full potential of your French Door Air Fryer Oven. From quick weeknight dinners to elaborate feasts, these recipes are designed to inspire creativity in your kitchen. You'll discover how to prepare healthier versions of your favorite fried foods with little to no oil, as well as explore new dishes that take advantage of the oven's unique capabilities.

Each recipe has been tested and refined to ensure success, providing you with detailed instructions and tips to help you achieve perfect results every time. Whether you're in the mood for a savory roast, a batch of crispy fries, or a decadent dessert, this cookbook has something for everyone. So, let's get started—unlock the full potential of your Emeril Lagasse French Door Air Fryer Oven and elevate your cooking to the next level!

This is a stylish device that combines multiple cooking functions in one. Designed with 24 preset functions, this oven allows you to air fry, bake, roast, broil and more with ease. Its unique French door design enhances both style and functionality, providing easy access without taking up extra space. The oven's intuitive controls and user-friendly interface make it easy for anyone to cook delicious and healthy food quickly. It features even heat distribution and energy efficiency, changing the landscape of the modern kitchen.

The Emeril Lagasse French Door Air Fryer Oven is a versatile and innovative kitchen appliance that combines the functionalities of an air fryer, convection oven, toaster, and dehydrator into one sleek and efficient unit. Designed with the expertise of celebrity chef Emeril Lagasse, this appliance features a unique French door design, which not only adds a touch of elegance to your kitchen but also provides easy access to your food, allowing you to monitor the cooking process effortlessly.

This powerful appliance is equipped with 24 custom presets that cater to a wide range of cooking needs, from air frying and baking to broiling and dehydrating. The advanced heating elements and fan deliver consistent and even cooking, ensuring your meals come out perfectly every time. Whether you're looking to prepare crispy fries with little to no oil, roast a tender chicken, or bake a batch of cookies, the Emeril Lagasse French Door Air Fryer Oven has you covered.

With its spacious interior, this air fryer oven can accommodate large meals, making it ideal for families and entertaining. Plus, its easy-to-use digital controls and dishwasher-safe parts make cooking and cleanup a breeze. Elevate your cooking experience with the Emeril Lagasse French Door Air Fryer Oven.

Functions of the Emeril Lagasse French Door Air Fryer Oven

The Emeril Lagasse French Door Air Fryer Oven comes with 24 preset functions designed to make cooking more efficient and versatile. With presets for everything from fries and bacon to rotisserie chicken and pastries, the oven takes the guesswork out of cooking, ensuring perfectly prepared dishes every time. Additionally, its defrost, reheat, and keep-warm functions allow for extra convenience when handling leftovers or frozen foods. The slow cook and dehydrate options further enhance its functionality, letting you simmer stews or create healthy snacks like dried fruits and jerky. Designed with ease of use and efficiency in mind, the Emeril Lagasse French Door Air Fryer Oven simplifies mealtime and maximizes your cooking potential, making it an indispensable tool in any modern kitchen.

1. **Airfry:** Cook crispy foods using little to no oil.
2. **Fries:** Make golden, crunchy French fries easily.
3. **Bacon:** Crisp up bacon without excess grease.
4. **Grill:** Perfect for grilling meats and vegetables indoors.
5. **Eggs:** Cook eggs to your liking for breakfast.
6. **Fish:** Prepare tender and moist fish dishes.
7. **Ribs:** Slow-cook ribs for a tender, fall-off-the-bone finish.
8. **Defrost:** Safely and evenly defrost frozen food.
9. **Steak:** Cook steak to your preferred doneness with ease.
10. **Vegetables:** Roast or air fry vegetables for a healthy side.
11. **Wings:** Make perfectly crispy and flavorful chicken wings.
12. **Bake:** Bake cakes, bread, and other pastries with even heat.
13. **Rotisserie:** Cook whole chickens or roasts with rotating, self-basting heat.

14. **Toast:** Toast bread evenly for breakfast or snacks.

15. **Chicken:** Roast whole chickens with crispy skin and juicy meat.

16. **Pizza:** Achieve crispy crusts and melted cheese for homemade pizza.

17. **Pastry:** Bake delicate pastries with precision.

18. **Proof:** Perfect setting for proofing dough for baking.

19. **Broil:** Brown and caramelize the top of your dishes.

20. **Slow Cook:** Simmer stews, soups, and braises over time.

21. **Roast:** Roast meats and vegetables to perfection.

22. **Dehydrate:** Create healthy snacks like dried fruit and jerky.

23. **Reheat:** Warm leftovers without drying them out.

24. **Warm:** Keep food warm until it's time to serve, ensuring it stays at the perfect temperature.

These features allow you to tackle a wide variety of cooking tasks, making the Emeril Lagasse French Door Air Fryer

Oven a highly versatile appliance in any kitchen.

Benefits of Using It

The Emeril Lagasse French Door Air Fryer Oven offers numerous benefits that make it an essential kitchen appliance for those looking to enhance their cooking experience. With its wide range of functions and features, this versatile oven can replace multiple kitchen gadgets, saving time, space, and energy. Here are the key benefits of using this innovative appliance:

1. Versatile Cooking Options

With 24 preset cooking functions, the Emeril Lagasse French Door Air Fryer Oven allows you to air fry, bake, roast, grill, toast, and more, all in one unit. Whether you want to cook crispy fries, juicy rotisserie chicken, or perfectly baked pizza, this appliance can do it all. It's designed to cater to various cooking needs, making it ideal for any meal, whether breakfast, lunch, or dinner.

2. Healthier Cooking

One of the standout features is the air fry function, which allows you to enjoy your favorite fried foods with little to no oil. This significantly reduces the calorie and fat content of your meals while still delivering crispy, delicious results. By using hot air circulation, the oven promotes healthier cooking without sacrificing flavor.

3. Efficient and Time-Saving

The convection fan technology in the oven ensures even heat distribution, meaning your meals cook faster than in traditional ovens. With its ability to heat up quickly and cook food evenly, this appliance saves you time, whether you're preparing a quick weeknight dinner or a more elaborate meal for family and friends.

4. User-Friendly Design

The French door design allows for easy access to the oven, making it simple to check on your food without the risk of burning yourself. Additionally, the digital display and intuitive control panel make it easy to select and customize cooking settings. The oven's large capacity also means you can cook multiple dishes at once, making meal preparation for large families or gatherings a breeze.

5. Energy Efficient

The Emeril Lagasse French Door Air Fryer Oven uses less energy than traditional ovens, thanks to its advanced heating and air circulation technology. This not only reduces your utility bills but also makes it an eco-friendly option for energy-conscious consumers.

6. Space-Saving and Multi-Functional

Instead of having separate appliances for air frying, baking, roasting, and grilling, this all-in-one oven combines all these functions in one sleek unit. Its compact design makes it a perfect fit for any kitchen, especially for those with limited counter space.

7. Perfect for Any Culinary Level

Whether you're a seasoned chef or a beginner, the preset functions and easy-to-use controls make this oven accessible to anyone. It takes the guesswork out of cooking, allowing you to produce restaurant-quality meals at home with minimal effort.

In summary, the Emeril Lagasse French Door Air Fryer Oven is a game-changing appliance that simplifies cooking, enhances meal quality, and promotes healthier eating. Its versatility, convenience, and energy efficiency make it a valuable addition to any kitchen.

Before First Use

Before you start cooking with your Emeril Lagasse French Door Air Fryer Oven, it's essential to follow a few simple steps to ensure optimal performance and safety. Here's a quick guide to get you started:

1. Unpack and Inspect: Carefully remove the oven from its packaging and inspect it for any visible damage. Ensure that all accessories, such as the Crisper Tray, Rotisserie Spit, Baking Pan, and others, are included.

2. Clean the Oven: Wipe down the interior and exterior of the oven with a damp cloth. Wash all removable accessories, such as the Crisper Tray, Baking Pan, and Wire Rack, with warm, soapy water. Rinse thoroughly and dry before placing them back in the oven.

3. Position the Oven: Place the oven on a flat, heat-resistant surface with ample space around it for ventilation. Ensure that the oven is not placed near flammable materials and that the French doors can open fully without obstruction.

4. Initial Preheat: Before cooking your

first meal, it's recommended to run the oven empty for about 10 minutes. Set it to a high temperature (e.g., 400°F) and select the Air Fry function. This will help burn off any residue from the manufacturing process and eliminate any initial odors.

5. Familiarize Yourself with the Controls: Take a few moments to explore the control panel and understand the different pre-set functions. Familiarizing yourself with the settings will make your cooking experience smoother and more enjoyable.

Following these steps will ensure that your Emeril Lagasse French Door Air Fryer Oven is ready for use and that you're set up for success in the kitchen.

Using the Emeril Lagasse French Door Air Fryer Oven is straightforward and user-friendly. Follow these step-by-step instructions to get the most out of your versatile appliance:

1. Setting Up the Oven

Before using the oven, ensure that it's placed on a stable, heat-resistant surface with ample space around it for ventilation. Plug the oven into an electrical outlet. Make sure that the interior racks and accessories, such as the crisper tray or baking pan, are properly positioned according to the dish you plan to cook.

2. Preheating the Oven (If Needed)

For certain dishes, preheating the oven may be necessary. If your recipe calls for preheating, press the appropriate cooking function button (e.g., Bake, Air Fry, Broil) and set the desired temperature. Allow the oven to heat up for about 5–10 minutes, depending on the function. The oven's digital display will indicate when it reaches the set temperature.

3. Selecting the Cooking Function

The Emeril Lagasse French Door Air Fryer Oven comes with 24 preset cooking functions. To select a cooking function, simply press the function button that corresponds to your dish—such as Airfry, Bake, Grill, or Toast. You can scroll through the options using the function knob or control panel. Once you've selected the function, use the temperature and time adjustment buttons to customize your cooking parameters.

4. Placing Your Food

Once the oven is preheated (if necessary), place your food on the appropriate tray or pan. For air frying, use the crisper tray, which allows hot air to circulate around your food for even cooking. If you're baking, roasting, or toasting, you can place your dish on the wire rack or baking pan. Close the French doors gently to avoid letting too much heat escape.

5. Adjusting Time and Temperature

After selecting your cooking function, use the time and temperature knobs to set the desired cooking time and temperature. The oven allows precise control over these settings, which helps to ensure perfectly cooked meals. Most recipes will provide specific time and temperature guidelines, but you can adjust them as needed based on your preferences.

6. Monitoring the Cooking Process

The large glass French doors and internal light allow you to easily monitor your food without opening the oven, helping to retain heat and ensure even cooking. You can pause or stop the cooking process by pressing the Start/Pause button at any time.

7. Finishing and Removing Food

Once the cooking time is complete, the oven will beep to signal that your meal is ready. Use oven mitts to carefully remove your food from the oven, as the trays and racks will be hot. If your food needs more time, you can add additional minutes by adjusting the time setting without needing to preheat again.

8. Cleaning Up

Once the oven has cooled, use a damp cloth to wipe down the interior for cleaning. Remove the racks and trays and wash them with warm soapy water or place them in the dishwasher if they're dishwasher-safe. Ensure the oven is completely dry before storing it.

By following these steps, you'll be able to fully enjoy the Emeril Lagasse French Door Air Fryer Oven, preparing delicious and perfectly cooked meals every time.

Here are some tips for using the accessories of the Emeril Lagasse French Door Air Fryer Oven to enhance your cooking experience and ensure optimal results:

1. Drip Tray

Best for: Catching grease and drippings from food cooked in the crisper tray, grill plate, or rotisserie.

Tip: Always place the drip tray on the lowest rack position when air frying, grilling, or using the rotisserie to prevent oil or drippings from dirtying the oven.

Tip: Line the drip tray with foil for easier cleaning, especially when cooking fatty or greasy foods.

2. Wire Rack

Best for: Baking, toasting, or roasting foods.

Tip: Place the wire rack in different positions depending on what you're cooking. For baking or roasting, use the middle position, and for broiling or toasting, use the top rack.

Tip: Be cautious not to overload the wire rack to ensure proper air circulation and even cooking.

3. Baking Pan

Best for: Baking, roasting, or reheating.

Tip: Use the baking pan for roasting vegetables, baking casseroles, or reheating leftovers. It works well for catching juices when roasting meats.

Tip: For easier cleanup, consider lining the baking pan with parchment paper or aluminum foil, especially when cooking foods that may stick.

4. Rotisserie Spit

Best for: Rotisserie-style cooking of whole chickens, turkey breasts, or other meats.

Tip: Insert the rotisserie spit through the center of the meat, securing it with the forks at both ends. Ensure the food is evenly balanced on the spit to prevent wobbling during cooking.

Tip: Always use the fetch tool to remove the rotisserie spit after cooking to avoid burning yourself.

5. Crisper Tray

Best for: Air frying or crisping foods like fries, wings, or vegetables.

Tip: Place food in a single layer on the crisper tray for even air circulation and crisping. Be sure not to overcrowd, as this hinders proper air circulation.

Tip: Rotate or shake the crisper tray halfway through cooking for uniform crispness.

6. Fetch Tool

Best for: Safely removing hot accessories like the rotisserie spit or crisper tray from the oven.

Tip: Use the fetch tool to securely grip the ends of the rotisserie spit or crisper tray handles when removing them from the oven, ensuring safety.

Tip: Keep the fetch tool nearby when using high-heat settings to avoid handling hot accessories directly.

7. Grill Plate

Best for: Grilling meats, fish, and vegetables.

Tip: Preheat the grill plate for a few minutes

before placing food on it to achieve grill marks and even cooking. Lightly oil the surface to prevent sticking.

Tip: Place the drip tray underneath to catch any grease or drippings from the grilling process.

8. Grill Plate Handle

Best for: Safely lifting and removing the grill plate from the oven.

Tip: Use the grill plate handle to securely lift and move the grill plate in and out of the oven, especially when it's hot.

Tip: Be cautious when handling the grill plate after cooking, as it will retain heat. Use oven mitts or the grill plate handle for safety.

By properly utilizing each accessory, you can maximize the versatility of your Emeril Lagasse French Door Air Fryer Oven and achieve excellent results with a wide variety of dishes.

Proper cleaning and maintenance of your Emeril Lagasse French Door Air Fryer Oven will ensure it remains in top working condition for years to come. Here's a step-by-step guide to help you care for your appliance:

1. Unplug and Cool Down:

Always unplug the oven and let it cool completely before starting the cleaning process to ensure safety.

2. Remove Accessories:

Take out all removable accessories, including the drip tray, wire rack, baking pan, Rotisserie Spit, Crisper Tray, Fetch Tool, Grill Plate, and Grill Plate Handle.

3. Clean the Interior:

Gently wipe the interior with a soft, damp cloth or sponge. For tougher stains, apply a mild dish soap solution. Avoid abrasive cleaners or scouring pads, as they may damage the interior surfaces.

4. Clean the Accessories:

Wash all removable accessories with warm, soapy water. Use a non-abrasive sponge or brush

to remove any food residue. Rinse thoroughly and dry completely before reassembling. Most accessories are dishwasher-safe, but it's best to consult the user manual to confirm. If dishwasher cleaning, place the items on the top rack.

5. Clean the Door and Exterior:
Wipe down the glass doors and the exterior of the oven with a damp cloth. For greasy spots, a mild detergent can be used. Be sure to dry the surfaces with a soft towel to prevent water spots or streaks.

6. Maintain the Heating Elements:

Gently wipe the heating elements with a damp cloth. Avoid using water directly on the elements or soaking them, as this can damage the oven.

7. Empty the Crumbs and Drip Tray:
Regularly check and empty the drip tray and crumb tray to prevent buildup. Clean these trays with warm, soapy water, rinse, and dry them thoroughly.

8. Regular Inspections:
Periodically check the oven for any signs of wear or damage, particularly around the door seals and heating elements. Address any

issues promptly to maintain optimal performance.

9. Storage:

When not in use, store your Emeril Lagasse French Door Air Fryer Oven in a cool, dry place. Ensure that it is unplugged and that all accessories are clean and dry before storing.

10. Routine Maintenance:

Perform a deep clean of your oven monthly if you use it regularly. This involves a thorough cleaning of all parts, ensuring that the oven remains hygienic and operates efficiently.

By following these simple steps, your Emeril Lagasse French Door Air Fryer Oven will continue to deliver delicious meals with ease, making it a reliable companion in your kitchen.

Frequently Asked Questions & Notes

1. What Are the Main Features of the Emeril Lagasse French Door Air Fryer Oven?

Answer: The Emeril Lagasse French Door Air Fryer Oven is a multifunctional kitchen appliance that combines air frying, baking, roasting, broiling, and more. It comes with 24 pre-set functions, allowing you to cook a wide variety of meals with ease. The French door design adds a touch of elegance and makes it convenient to open the oven without the need to remove it from the countertop.

2. How Do I Use the Air Fry Function?

Answer: To use the Air Fry function, select "Air Fry" on the control panel, then set your desired temperature and cooking time using the dial. Place your food on the Crisper Tray for best results. The Air Fry function circulates hot air around your food, giving it a crispy texture with little to no oil.

3. Can I Use Aluminum Foil in the Oven?

Answer: Yes, you can use aluminum foil in the Emeril Lagasse French Door Air Fryer Oven. However, make sure to leave space around the food for proper air circulation. Do not cover the Crisper Tray completely, as this can block airflow and affect cooking results.

4. How Do I Clean the Oven?

Answer: To clean the oven, unplug it and allow it to cool. Remove all accessories, such as the drip tray and racks, and wash them with warm, soapy water. Wipe down the interior and exterior with a damp cloth. Avoid using abrasive cleaners or scouring pads, as they can damage the surfaces.

5. What Should I Do If My Oven Is Not Heating Properly?

Answer: If your oven is not heating properly, check to ensure it is plugged in and that the door is securely closed. If the issue persists, contact Emeril Lagasse customer support for assistance, as it may require a professional inspection.

6. Can I Cook Multiple Items at Once?

Answer: Yes, the oven is designed to cook multiple items simultaneously, thanks to its large capacity and versatile rack system. You can use different levels of the oven to prepare various dishes at the same time, making it perfect for family meals or entertaining guests.

7. What Accessories Are Included?

Answer: The Emeril Lagasse French Door Air Fryer Oven comes with several accessories, including a Crisper Tray, Baking Pan, Wire Rack, Rotisserie Spit, and Fetch Tool. Each accessory is designed to enhance your cooking experience and help you achieve the best results.

8. Is the Oven Energy Efficient?

Answer: Yes, the Emeril Lagasse French Door Air Fryer Oven is designed to be energy-efficient, using less power than traditional ovens while still delivering fast and even cooking results.

Notes

Preheating: Some recipes may require preheating the oven. Always refer to the recipe instructions for best results.

Safety: Always use oven mitts when handling hot accessories and food items. The exterior and interior of the oven can become hot during use.

Placement: Ensure the oven is placed on a stable, heat-resistant surface with enough space around it for proper ventilation.

These FAQs and notes are designed to help you get the most out of your Emeril Lagasse French Door Air Fryer Oven, ensuring a seamless and enjoyable cooking experience.

4-Week Meal Plan

Week 1

Day 1:
Breakfast: Bell Pepper Egg Cups
Lunch: Beef Hot Dog Pizza
Snack: Bacon Wrapped Onion Rings
Dinner: Crisp Parmesan Chicken with Marinara Sauce
Dessert: Cream Cheese Coconut Pound Cake

Day 2:
Breakfast: Delicious Mozzarella-Pepperoni Rolls
Lunch: Fluffy Cheese Yogurt Muffins
Snack: Aromatic Brussels Sprout
Dinner: Cheese Pepperoni Bread Pockets
Dessert: Sweet Creamy Plum

Day 3:
Breakfast: Breakfast Eggplant-Spinach Frittata
Lunch: Roasted Radishes with Goat Cheese
Snack: Buttered Cheese Apple Rollups
Dinner: Parmesan-Crusted Snapper Fillets with Almond Sauce
Dessert: Homemade Coconut Cookies

Day 4:
Breakfast: Cheesy Leek Omelet
Lunch: Prosciutto-Wrapped Asparagus
Snack: Five-Spiced Chicken Wings
Dinner: Spicy Almond-Crusted Chicken Breasts
Dessert: Apple Pies

Day 5:
Breakfast: Baby Spinach Cheese Muffins
Lunch: Refreshing Lemony Fennel
Snack: Crispy Rice Logs
Dinner: Pizza Tortilla Rolls
Dessert: Granola Bark

Day 6:
Breakfast: Crisp Bacon-Wrapped Eggs
Lunch: Roasted Bell Peppers
Snack: Radish Chips
Dinner: Minty Basil Shrimps
Dessert: Delicious Chocolate-Hazelnut Croissants

Day 7:
Breakfast: Minty Garlic Cheese Stuffed Mushrooms
Lunch: Spaghetti Squash with Avocado Carbonara
Snack: Ranch Cashew Bowls
Dinner: Easy Air Fried Pork Chops
Dessert: Dried Tart Cherries-Pecan Stuffed Apples

Week 2

Day 1:
Breakfast: Cheese Peppers Omelet
Lunch: Parmesan Cauliflower
Snack: Spinach Pie
Dinner: Palatable Pesto Chicken Legs
Dessert: Soft Blackberry Almond Cake

Day 2:
Breakfast: Coconut Muffins
Lunch: Creamy Cheese Cauliflower & Rutabaga
Snack: Herbed Olive Dip
Dinner: Meat & Vegetables Egg Rolls
Dessert: Cinnamon Plums

Day 3:
Breakfast: Baked Cheese Veggie and Eggs
Lunch: Garlic Green Beans with Bacon
Snack: Nutty Chicken, Berries and Spinach Bowls
Dinner: Herbed Honey Halibut Steaks
Dessert: Chocolate Berries Coconut Milk

Day 4:
Breakfast: Cheesy Cauliflower, Asparagus & Mushroom Casserole
Lunch: Chili Kabocha Squash
Snack: Bacon-Wrapped Chicken
Dinner: Lemon-Chili Chicken Drumsticks
Dessert: Fluffy Chocolate Soufflés

Day 5:
Breakfast: Roasted Veggies with Italian Sausage & Eggs
Lunch: Parmesan Eggplant Mash
Snack: Balsamic Tomato Mozzarella Salad
Dinner: Sesame Pork Cutlets with Aloha Salsa
Dessert: Banana Bread Pudding

Day 6:
Breakfast: Mini Breakfast Pepperoni Pizza Cups
Lunch: Aromatic Broccoli with Scallions
Snack: Cauliflower Popcorn
Dinner: Aromatic Cheesy Shrimps
Dessert: Apple Crumble

Day 7:
Breakfast: Flavorful Cheese Chicken Sausage Frittata
Lunch: Nutty Cauliflower and Prosciutto Mix
Snack: Zucchini and Tomato Salsa
Dinner: Classic Sloppy Joes
Dessert: Goji Coffee Surprise with Flaxseed

Week 3

Day 1:
Breakfast: Cheesy Kale-Eggplant Omelet
Lunch: Flavorful Rutabaga with Cheddar
Snack: Spiced Pork Sticks
Dinner: Greek Cheese Chicken-Spinach Meatballs
Dessert: Chocolate Molten Cupcakes

Day 2:
Breakfast: Scrambled Cheese Eggs with Turkey Bacon
Lunch: Hot Lemony Cauliflower
Snack: Italian Popcorn Chicken
Dinner: Cheese Sausage Calzone
Dessert: Raspberry Chocolate Pudding

Day 3:
Breakfast: Cheese Beef Tomato Omelet
Lunch: Coconut Jicama Fries
Snack: Yummy Parmesan Pecan Balls
Dinner: Salmon Cakes
Dessert: Puff Pastry Apples

Day 4:
Breakfast: Cod Frittata
Lunch: Jarlsberg Cheese Roasted Cauliflower & Broccoli
Snack: Mini Chicken Wontons
Dinner: Crispy Spicy Chicken Strips
Dessert: Sweet Creamy Plum

Day 5:
Breakfast: Egg and Halibut Keto Rolls
Lunch: Delicious Parmesan Zucchini Noodles
Snack: Basil Salmon Bites
Dinner: Steak Fingers
Dessert: Cream Cheese Coconut Pound Cake

Day 6:
Breakfast: Flavorful Parmesan Steak Fingers
Lunch: Herbed Garlicky Broccoli Steaks
Snack: Eggplant Slices
Dinner: Lemon-Butter Sea Scallops
Dessert: Homemade Coconut Cookies

Day 7:
Breakfast: Bell Pepper Egg Cups
Lunch: Fluffy Cheese Yogurt Muffins
Snack: Bacon Wrapped Onion Rings
Dinner: Coconut Beef Steak
Dessert: Apple Pies

Week 4

Day 1:
Breakfast: Breakfast Eggplant-Spinach Frittata
Lunch: Roasted Radishes with Goat Cheese
Snack: Aromatic Brussels Sprout
Dinner: Flavorful Italian Chicken Thighs
Dessert: Raspberry Cheesecake

Day 2:
Breakfast: Baby Spinach Cheese Muffins
Lunch: Beef Hot Dog Pizza
Snack: Buttered Cheese Apple Rollups
Dinner: Mushroom and Bacon Stuffed Beef Roll
Dessert: Cinnamon Plums

Day 3:
Breakfast: Delicious Mozzarella-Pepperoni Rolls
Lunch: Prosciutto-Wrapped Asparagus
Snack: Crispy Rice Logs
Dinner: Swordfish and Cherry Tomato Skewers
Dessert: Dried Tart Cherries-Pecan Stuffed Apples

Day 4:
Breakfast: Cheesy Leek Omelet
Lunch: Refreshing Lemony Fennel
Snack: Five-Spiced Chicken Wings
Dinner: Turkey Breast with Mashed Strawberry
Dessert: Granola Bark

Day 5:
Breakfast: Crisp Bacon-Wrapped Eggs
Lunch: Spaghetti Squash with Avocado Carbonara
Snack: Radish Chips
Dinner: Tasty BBQ Beef Steaks
Dessert: Delicious Chocolate-Hazelnut Croissants

Day 6:
Breakfast: Coconut Muffins
Lunch: Creamy Cheese Cauliflower & Rutabaga
Snack: Ranch Cashew Bowls
Dinner: Coconut-Shrimp Po' Boys
Dessert: Goji Coffee Surprise with Flaxseed

Day 7:
Breakfast: Baked Cheese Veggie and Eggs
Lunch: Garlic Green Beans with Bacon
Snack: Cauliflower Popcorn
Dinner: Lamb-Cauliflower Fritters
Dessert: Banana Bread Pudding

Chapter 1 Breakfast

Roasted Veggies with Italian Sausage & Eggs

Prep Time: 10 minutes | Cook Time: 25 minutes | Servings: 4

1 pound Italian sausage

2 sprigs rosemary

1 celery, sliced

½ pound broccoli, cut into small florets

2 sprigs thyme

1 bell pepper, trimmed and cut into matchsticks

2 garlic cloves, smashed

2 tablespoons extra-virgin olive oil

1 leek, cut into halves lengthwise

A pinch of grated nutmeg

Salt and black pepper, to taste

4 whole eggs

1. Place the vegetables on the bottom of the baking pan. 2. Sprinkle with the seasonings and add the sausage on top. 3. Slide the baking pan into shelf position 6. 4. Select the Roast setting. Set the temperature to 375°F and the time to 20 minutes. Press Start/Pause to begin cooking, stirring occasionally. 5. When cooking time is up, top with eggs and lower the temperature to 330°F. Roast for 5 to 6 minutes more. Bon appétit!

Scrambled Cheese Eggs with Turkey Bacon

Prep Time: 10 minutes | Cook Time: 20 minutes | Servings: 4

½ pound turkey bacon

4 eggs

⅓ cup milk

2 tablespoons yogurt

½ teaspoon sea salt

1 bell pepper, finely chopped

2 green onions, finely chopped

½ cup Colby cheese, shredded

1. Place the turkey bacon in the crisper tray. Slide the Crisper Tray into shelf position 4/5. Select the Airfry setting. Set the temperature to 360°F and the time to 10 minutes. Press Start/Pause to begin cooking. 2. Remove and set the fried bacon aside. 3. In a bowl, whisk the eggs with milk and yogurt. Add salt, green onions and bell pepper. 4. Brush the sides and bottom of the baking pan with the reserved bacon grease.

Pour the egg mixture into the baking pan. Slide the Crisper Tray into shelf position 4/5. Air fry at 355°F for about 5 minutes. 5. Then top with the shredded Colby cheese and cook for 5 to 6 minutes more. 6. Serve the scrambled eggs with the reserved bacon.

Flavorful Cheese Chicken Sausage Frittata

Prep Time: 15 minutes | Cook Time: 11 minutes | Servings: 2

1 tablespoon olive oil

2 chicken sausages, sliced

4 eggs

1 garlic clove, minced

½ yellow onion, chopped

Sea salt and ground black pepper, to taste

4 tablespoons Monterey-Jack cheese

1 tablespoon fresh parsley leaves, chopped

1. Grease the sides and bottom of the baking pan with olive oil. 2. Place the sausages in the pan. Slide the baking pan into shelf position 4/5. Select the Airfry setting. Set the temperature to 360°F and the time to 5 minutes. Press Start/Pause to begin cooking. 3. Meanwhile, whisk the eggs with garlic and onion in a bowl. Season with salt and pepper. 4. Pour the mixture over the cooked sausages and spread the cheese on top. Cook at 360°F for an additional 6 minutes. 5. Sprinkle with fresh parsley leaves and serve.

Cheesy Cauliflower, Asparagus & Mushroom Casserole

Prep Time: 15 minutes | Cook Time: 20 minutes | Servings: 2

1 cup cauliflower rice

⅓ cup milk

⅓ cup Colby cheese, grated

1½ cups white mushrooms, sliced

2 asparagus spears, chopped

1 teaspoon table salt, or to taste

2 well-beaten eggs

⅓ teaspoon smoked cayenne pepper

1 teaspoon ground black pepper, or to taste

⅓ teaspoon dried rosemary, crushed

1. Place the cauliflower rice in the baking pan. 2. In a bowl, whisk together the eggs and milk. Stir in ½ of cheese and the seasonings. Pour ¾ of egg-cheese mixture over the cauliflower rice in the baking pan and press gently with a wide spatula. 3. Then, spread the mushrooms and chopped asparagus on top. Pour the remaining egg-cheese mixture over the top and spread it evenly. 4. Top with the remaining cheese. Slide the baking pan into shelf position 4/5. Select the Bake setting. Set the temperature to 325°F and the time to 20 minutes. Press Start/Pause to begin cooking.

Breakfast Eggplant-Spinach Frittata

Prep Time: 5 minutes | Cook Time: 20 minutes | Servings: 4

1 tablespoon chives, chopped

1 eggplant, cubed

8 ounces spinach, torn

Cooking spray

6 eggs, whisked

Salt and black pepper to the taste

1. In a medium bowl, whisk the eggs with the remaining ingredients except the cooking spray. Grease the baking pan with cooking spray, pour the frittata mix to the pan. 2. Slide the Crisper Tray into shelf position 4/5. Select the Airfry setting. Set the temperature to 380°F and the time to 20 minutes. Press Start/Pause to begin cooking. 3. Divide between plates and serve for breakfast.

Delicious Mozzarella-Pepperoni Rolls

Prep Time: 15 minutes | Cook Time: 6 minutes | Servings: 6

6 wonton wrappers

1 tablespoon keto tomato sauce

½ cup Mozzarella, shredded

1 oz. pepperoni, chopped

1 egg, beaten

Cooking spray

1. In a large bowl, combine the pepperoni, shredded Mozzarella, and tomato sauce. Stir until the mixture is homogenous place it onto the wonton wraps. Wrap the wonton wraps in the shape of sticks. Brush them with beaten eggs. 2. Spray the Crisper Tray with cooking spray. Place the Mozzarella rolls in the Crisper Tray. Slide the Crisper Tray into shelf position 4/5. Select the Airfry setting. Set the temperature to 400°F and the time to 3 minutes. Press Start/Pause to begin cooking. 3. After 3 minutes, press the Start/Pause button and flip them. Then press the Start/Pause Button again to continue cooking.

Cheese Beef Tomato Omelet

Prep Time: 10 minutes | Cook Time: 20 minutes | Servings: 3

1 teaspoon lard

⅔ pound ground beef

¼ teaspoon chili powder

½ teaspoon ground bay leaf

½ teaspoon ground pepper

Sea salt, to taste

1 green bell pepper, seeded and chopped

1 red bell pepper, seeded and chopped

6 eggs

⅓ cup double cream

½ cup Colby cheese, shredded

1 tomato, sliced

1. In a skillet over medium-high heat, melt the lard. Add the ground beef; cook for 4 minutes or until no longer pink, crumbling with a spatula. 2. Add the ground beef mixture, the spices and bell peppers to the baking pan. 3. In a bowl, whisk the eggs with double cream. Spoon the mixture over the meat and peppers in the baking pan. 4. Slide the pan into shelf position 4/5. Select the Airfry setting. Set the temperature to 355°F and the time to 10 minutes. Press Start/Pause to begin cooking. 5. When cooking time is up, top with the cheese and tomato slices. Cook for an additional 5 minutes or until the eggs are golden and the cheese has melted.

Baby Spinach Cheese Muffins

Prep Time: 5 minutes | Cook Time: 15 minutes | Servings: 4

2 eggs, whisked

Cooking spray

1 and ½ cups coconut milk

1 tablespoon baking powder

4 ounces baby spinach, chopped

2 ounces parmesan cheese, grated

3 ounces almond flour

1. In a bowl, mix together all the ingredients except the cooking spray. Grease a muffin pan that fits the French Door air fryer with cooking spray. Divide the muffins mix into the muffin pan. 2. Slide the Wire Rack into shelf position 4/5. Place the muffin pan on the Wire Rack. Select the Airfry setting. Set the temperature to 380°F and the time to 15 minutes. Press Start/Pause to begin cooking. 3. Divide between plates and serve.

Cod Frittata

Prep Time: 10 minutes | Cook Time: 20 minutes | Servings: 3

2 cod fillets

6 eggs

½ cup milk

½ teaspoon red pepper flakes, crushed

1 shallot, chopped

2 garlic cloves, minced

Sea salt and ground black pepper, to taste

1. Fill a pot with salted water and bring to a boil. Add the cod fillets and boil for 5 minutes or until it is opaque. Then flake the fish into bite-sized pieces. 2. In a bowl, whisk together the eggs and milk. Stir in the garlic, shallots, black pepper, salt, and red pepper flakes. Stir in the reserved fish. 3. Lightly grease a baking pan and pour the mixture inside. 4. Slide the pan into shelf position 4/5. Select the Airfry setting. Set the temperature to 360°F and the time to 9 minutes. Press Start/Pause to begin cooking. Flip it over halfway through the cooking process. Bon appétit!

Coconut Muffins

Prep Time: 10 minutes | Cook Time: 10 minutes | Servings: 2

⅓ cup almond flour

2 tablespoons Erythritol

¼ teaspoon baking powder

1 teaspoon apple cider vinegar

1 tablespoon coconut milk

1 tablespoon coconut oil, softened

1 teaspoon ground cinnamon

Cooking spray

1. In a mixing bowl, combine the almond flour, baking powder, Erythritol, and ground cinnamon and mix well. Add coconut milk, apple cider vinegar, and coconut oil and stir the mixture until smooth. 2. Spray the muffin molds with cooking spray and scoop the muffin batter in the muffin molds. Scrape the top of each muffin with a spatula. 3. Slide the Wire Rack into shelf position 4/5. Place the muffins on the Wire Rack. Select the Bake setting. Set the temperature to 365°F and the time to 10 minutes. Press Start/Pause to begin cooking. 4. Serve warm.

Crisp Bacon-Wrapped Eggs

Prep Time: 15 minutes | Cook Time: 5 minutes | Servings: 2

2 eggs, hard-boiled, peeled

4 bacon slices

½ teaspoon avocado oil

1 teaspoon mustard

1. Spray the Crisper Tray with avocado oil and place the bacon slices inside in one layer. 2. Slide the Crisper Tray into shelf position 4/5. Select the Airfry setting. Set the temperature to 400°F and the time to 4 minutes. Press Start/Pause to begin cooking. Flip the bacon halfway through the cooking time. 3. Once done, allow the bacon to cool to the room temperature. Wrap each egg in two slices of bacon. 4. Secure the eggs with toothpicks and place them in the Crisper Tray. Cook the wrapped eggs for one minute at 400°F.

Cheese Peppers Omelet

Prep Time: 5 minutes | Cook Time: 20 minutes | Servings: 4

½ cup cheddar cheese, shredded

2 tablespoons chives, chopped

A pinch of salt and black pepper

¼ cup coconut cream

1 cup red bell peppers, chopped

Cooking spray

1. In a bowl, combine all the ingredients except the cooking spray and mix well. Grease the baking pan with cooking spray and pour the mixture into it. 2. Slide the baking pan into shelf position 4/5. Select the Airfry setting. Set the temperature to 360°F and the time to 20 minutes. Press Start/Pause to begin cooking. 3. Once done cooking, divide between plates and serve for breakfast.

Cheesy Kale-Eggplant Omelet

Prep Time: 10 minutes | Cook Time: 20 minutes | Servings: 4

1 eggplant, cubed

4 eggs, whisked

2 teaspoons cilantro, chopped

Salt and black pepper to the taste

½ teaspoon Italian seasoning

Cooking spray

½ cup kale, chopped

2 tablespoons cheddar, grated

2 tablespoons fresh basil, chopped

1. Place all the ingredients to a bowl except the cooking spray and whisk well. Grease the baking pan with cooking spray and pour the eggs mix into the pan. 2. Slide the baking pan into shelf position 4/5. Select the Airfry setting. Set the temperature to 370°F and the time to 20 minutes. Press Start/Pause to begin cooking. 3. Divide the mix between plates and serve.

Baked Cheese Veggie and Eggs

Prep Time: 5 minutes | Cook Time: 30 minutes | Servings: 6

Cooking spray

2 cups green and red bell pepper, chopped

2 spring onions, chopped

1 teaspoon thyme, chopped

Salt and black pepper to the taste

1 cup coconut cream

4 eggs, whisked

1 cup cheddar cheese, grated

Whisk together all the ingredients in a bowl except the cooking spray and the cheese. Grease the baking pan with cooking spray. Pour the bell pepper mixture into the pan and sprinkle the cheese on top.

Slide the baking pan into shelf position 4/5. Select the Bake setting. Set the temperature to 350°F and the time to 30 minutes. Press Start/Pause to begin cooking.

Divide between plates and serve.

Minty Garlic Cheese Stuffed Mushrooms

Prep Time: 10 minutes | Cook Time: 12 minutes | Servings: 3

2 garlic cloves, minced

1 teaspoon ground black pepper, plus more to taste

½ teaspoon paprika

1 teaspoon dried parsley flakes

1½ tablespoons fresh mint, chopped

1 teaspoon salt, or more to taste

1 cup Gruyère cheese, shredded

9 large mushrooms, cleaned, stalks removed

1. To prepare the filling, in a bowl, mix all of the ingredients except the mushrooms. 2. Stuff the mushrooms with the prepared filling and place them in the Crisper Tray. Slide the Crisper Tray into shelf position 4/5. Select the Airfry setting. Set the temperature to 375°F and the time to 12 minutes. Press Start/Pause to begin cooking. 3. Serve as an appetizer.

Mini Breakfast Pepperoni Pizza Cups

Prep Time: 10 minutes | Cook Time: 20 minutes | Servings: 4

12 slices pepperoni, 2-inch

2 tablespoons butter, melted

4 eggs, beaten

¼ teaspoon ground black pepper

Salt, to taste

4 slices smoked ham, chopped

1 cup mozzarella cheese, shredded

4 tablespoons ketchup

1. Lightly grease a muffin tin with nonstick spray and place the pepperoni inside. 2. In a mixing bowl, combine the remaining ingredients and divide among the muffins. 3. Slide the wire rack into shelf position 4/5. Place the muffin tin on the wire rack. Select the Bake. Set the temperature to 350°F and the time to 20 minutes. Press Start/Pause to begin cooking. 4. Bake until a toothpick inserted in the center and comes out clean. Let cool for 5 minutes before serving. Bon appétit!

Egg and Halibut Keto Rolls

Prep Time: 10 minutes | Cook Time: 20 minutes | Servings: 4

4 keto rolls

1 pound smoked halibut, chopped

4 eggs

1 teaspoon dried thyme

1 teaspoon dried basil

Salt and black pepper, to taste

1. Cut off the top of each keto roll and scoop out the insides to make the shells. 2. Arrange the prepared keto roll shells in the lightly greased baking pan. 3. Spray with cooking oil and add the halibut. Crack an egg into each keto roll shell and sprinkle with basil, thyme, salt, and black pepper. 4. Slide the baking pan into shelf position 4/5. Select the Bake setting. Set the temperature to 325°F and the time to 20 minutes. Press Start/Pause to begin cooking. Bon appétit!

Flavorful Parmesan Steak Fingers

Prep Time: 10 minutes | Cook Time: 14 minutes | Servings: 4

2 eggs, beaten

4 tablespoons yogurt

1 cup parmesan cheese, grated

1 teaspoon dry mesquite flavored seasoning mix

Coarse salt and ground black pepper, to taste

½ teaspoon onion powder

1-pound cube steak, cut into 3-inch-long strips

1. In a shallow bowl, whisk the eggs and yogurt. In a resealable bag, combine the parmesan cheese, salt, pepper, mesquite seasoning, and onion powder. 2. Firstly, dip the steak pieces in the egg mixture; then place in the bag and shake to coat on all sides. 3. Place the coated steak pieces in the Crisper Tray. Slide the Crisper Tray into shelf position 4/5. Select the Airfry setting. Set the temperature to 400°F and the time to 14 minutes. Press Start/Pause to begin cooking. 4. Flip halfway through the cooking process. 5. Serve with the vegetables to your liking.

Cheesy Leek Omelet

Prep Time: 5 minutes | Cook Time: 7 minutes | Servings: 2

2 leeks, chopped

4 eggs, whisked

¼ cup Cheddar cheese, shredded

½ cup Mozzarella cheese, shredded

1 teaspoon avocado oil

1. In a large bowl that fits in the appliance, whisk together the eggs with the remaining ingredients. 2. Slide the Wire Rack into shelf position 4/5. Place the bowl on the wire rack. 3. Select the Airfry setting. Set the temperature to 400°F and the time to 7 minutes. Press Start/ Pause to begin cooking. Serve warm.

Bell Pepper Egg Cups

Prep Time: 10 minutes | Cook Time: 4 minutes | Servings: 12

6 green bell peppers

12 egg

½ teaspoon ground black pepper

½ teaspoon chili flakes

1. Cut the bell peppers into halves and remove the seeds. 2. Crack the eggs in every bell pepper half and sprinkle with black pepper and chili flakes. 3. Place the green bell pepper halves in the Crisper Tray. Slide the Crisper Tray into shelf position 4/5. Select the Airfry setting. Set the temperature to 395°F and the time to 4 minutes. Press Start/Pause to begin cooking. Serve warm.

Chapter 2 Vegetables and Sides

Fluffy Cheese Yogurt Muffins

Prep Time: 10 minutes | Cook Time: 12 minutes | Servings: 4

1 cup almond flour

1 teaspoon dried dill

⅛ teaspoon salt

¼ teaspoon onion powder

2 teaspoons baking powder

1 large egg

¼ cup plain Greek yogurt

¼ cup grated Parmesan cheese

1. In a mixing bowl, combine the almond flour, salt, onion powder, dill, and baking powder. 2. In another bowl, whisk together the egg, Parmesan cheese and yogurt. Add the wet ingredients to dry ingredients and stir until well combined. 3. Lightly grease six silicone muffin cups with olive oil and divide the batter among them. 4. Slide the wire rack into shelf position 4/5. Place the muffin cups on the wire rack. Select the Airfry setting. Set the temperature to 350°F and the time to 12 minutes. Press Start/Pause to begin cooking. 5. Serve warm.

Beef Hot Dog Pizza

Prep Time: 5 minutes | Cook Time: 10 minutes | Servings: 4

½ cup finely ground almond flour

¼ cup arrowroot flour

1 tablespoon granular erythritol

½ teaspoon baking powder

¼ teaspoon salt

2 tablespoons butter, melted

1 tablespoon no-sugar-added tomato paste

1 large egg

½ teaspoon unflavored gelatin

1 teaspoon dried thyme

2 beef hot dogs, cut into ½" sections

1. In a bowl, combine the almond flour, arrowroot flour, baking powder, erythritol, and salt. 2. In a small bowl, whisk together the egg, butter, gelatin, tomato paste, and thyme. Add the butter mixture to the flour mixture and stir until smooth. Fold in the hot dogs. 3. Spoon mixture into a pizza pan that fits the device. 4. Slide the wire rack into shelf position 6. Select the Pizza setting. Set the temperature to 300°F and the time to 10 minutes. Press Start/Pause to begin cooking. 5. Slice and serve warm.

Roasted Radishes with Goat Cheese

Prep Time: 10 minutes | Cook Time: 10 minutes | Servings: 2

2 tablespoons butter, melted

2 cloves garlic, peeled and minced

¼ teaspoon salt

20 medium radishes, ends trimmed,

quartered

2 tablespoons goat cheese crumbles

1 tablespoon chopped fresh parsley

1. In a medium bowl, mix together the garlic, butter, and salt. Add in the radishes and toss well. 2. Place radishes in the crisper tray. Slide the Crisper Tray into shelf position 4/5. Select the Airfry setting. Set the temperature to 375°F and the time to 10 minutes. Press Start/Pause to begin cooking. Flip halfway through the cooking time. 3. Transfer the cooked radishes to a serving dish. Toss with goat cheese and garnish with parsley. Serve warm.

Parmesan Cauliflower

Prep Time: 10 minutes | Cook Time: 6 minutes | Servings: 4

3 tablespoons butter, melted

2 tablespoons grated Parmesan cheese

2 teaspoons dried thyme

½ teaspoon garlic powder

¼ teaspoon salt

1 large head cauliflower, chopped into small florets

1. Mix together the butter, garlic powder, thyme, Parmesan cheese, and salt in a large bowl. Stir in the cauliflower florets. 2. Place the cauliflower mixture in the crisper tray. Slide the Crisper Tray into shelf position 4/5. Select the Vegetables setting. Set the temperature to 350°F and the time to 6 minutes. Press Start/Pause to begin cooking. Flip them halfway through the cooking time. 3. Transfer cooked cauliflower to a serving bowl. Serve warm.

Creamy Cheese Cauliflower & Rutabaga

Prep Time: 10 minutes | Cook Time: 15 minutes | Servings: 4

1 small head cauliflower, chopped into small florets

1 medium rutabaga, peeled and small-diced

4 tablespoons butter, divided

1 teaspoon salt, divided

3 cloves garlic, peeled

½ teaspoon freshly ground black pepper

2 ounces cream cheese, room temperature

½ cup unsweetened almond milk

1. Place the cauliflower florets and rutabaga in a large bowl; toss with 2 tablespoons melted butter and ½ teaspoon salt. 2. Place the mixture in the crisper tray. Slide the Crisper Tray into shelf position 4/5. Select the Vegetables setting. Set the temperature to 350°F and the time to 10 minutes. Press Start/Pause to begin cooking. Toss them halfway through the cooking time. 3. Add the garlic and cook for another 5 minutes. 4. Using a stand blender, blend the cooked ingredients with remaining butter, salt, black pepper, cream cheese, and almond milk. 5. Transfer to a serving dish and serve warm.

Roasted Bell Peppers

Prep Time: 10 minutes | Cook Time: 24 minutes | Servings: 2

2 large red bell peppers, tops and bottoms removed, cut along rib sections and seeded

2 tablespoons olive oil

1. In a small bowl, toss the bell peppers with olive oil and transfer to the Crisper Tray. 2. Slide the Crisper Tray into shelf position 4/5. Select the Vegetables setting. Set the temperature to 400°F and the time to 24 minutes. Press Start/Pause to begin cooking. Flip them halfway through the cooking time. 3. Transfer the peppers to a small bowl and cover with plastic wrap. Let rest for 15 minutes. 4. Then remove the peppers from the bowl, peel off the skins and discard. Serve on a plate.

Prosciutto-Wrapped Asparagus

Prep Time: 10 minutes | Cook Time: 12 minutes | Servings: 4

3 ounces prosciutto, sliced lengthwise into 18 slices

18 thick asparagus spears, trimmed of woody ends

1. Spiral wrap the prosciutto strips from the bottom of the asparagus to the top, stopping just before covering the tip. 2. Place wrapped asparagus in the Crisper Tray. Slide the Crisper Tray into shelf position 4/5. Select the Airfry setting. Set the temperature to 400°F and the time to 12 minutes. Press Start/Pause to begin cooking. Flip halfway through the cooking time. 3. Transfer to a plate and serve.

Spaghetti Squash with Avocado Carbonara

Prep Time: 5 minutes | Cook Time: 32 minutes | Servings: 4

2 teaspoons olive oil

1 (1½-pound) spaghetti squash, halved and seeded

1 medium ripe avocado, peeled and pitted

¼ cup chicken broth

1 large egg

2 tablespoons grated Parmesan cheese

¼ teaspoon salt

2 slices sugar-free bacon

¼ cup chopped fresh parsley

1. Rub both halves of spaghetti squash with olive oil. Place flat sides down in the crisper tray. Slide the Crisper Tray into shelf position 4/5. Select the Airfry setting. Set the temperature to 375°F and the time to 25 minutes. Press Start/Pause to begin cooking. 2. In the mean time, in a medium bowl, blend together the avocado, egg, chicken broth, Parmesan cheese, and salt. Set aside. 3. In a skillet over medium heat, cook the bacon for 5 minutes until crispy. Transfer the cooked bacon to a paper towel to cool 5 minutes and crumble it. Set aside. 4. Transfer the cooked squash to a cutting board and cool for 5 minutes until easy to handle. Using a fork, gently pull the strands out of squash. Transfer the strands to the same skillet. 5. Add the avocado mixture and parsley to the skillet and cook them over medium heat. Toss the spaghetti squash with sauce until well coated, about 2 minutes. Stir in the bacon crumbles. 6. Transfer to a large serving bowl and serve warm.

Refreshing Lemony Fennel

Prep Time: 5 minutes | Cook Time: 8 minutes | Servings: 2

1 large fennel bulb, fronds removed and reserved, sliced

2 teaspoons olive oil

¼ teaspoon salt

2 lemon wedges

1 tablespoon chopped fennel fronds

1. Brush both sides of the fennel slices with olive oil and season with salt. 2. Place fennel slices in in the Crisper Tray. Slide the Crisper Tray into shelf position 4/5. Select the Vegetables setting. Set the temperature to 350°F and the time to 8 minutes. Press Start/Pause to begin cooking. 3. When cooking is complete, transfer to a serving dish. Squeeze with lemon and garnish with chopped fronds. Serve warm.

Garlic Green Beans with Bacon

Prep Time: 5 minutes | Cook Time: 10 minutes | Servings: 4

2 cups fresh green beans, ends trimmed

1 tablespoon butter, melted

½ teaspoon salt

¼ teaspoon freshly ground black pepper

1 slice sugar-free bacon, diced

1 clove garlic, peeled and minced

1 lemon wedge

1. In a medium bowl, toss the green beans with butter, salt, and black pepper. 2. Add green beans to the crisper tray. Slide the Crisper Tray into shelf position 4/5. Select the Vegetables setting. Set the temperature to 375°F and the time to 5 minutes. Press Start/Pause to begin cooking. 3. Stir in bacon and cook for 4 minutes longer. 4. Toss in minced garlic and cook for 1 more minute. 5. Transfer to a serving dish and squeeze with lemon. Toss well and serve warm.

Flavorful Rutabaga with Cheddar

Prep Time: 15 minutes | Cook Time: 8 minutes | Servings: 2

6 oz. rutabaga, chopped

2 oz. Cheddar cheese, grated

1 tablespoon coconut oil

½ teaspoon dried cilantro

½ teaspoon salt

½ teaspoon onion powder

3 tablespoons coconut cream

1. In a medium bowl, toss the rutabaga with coconut oil, salt, dried cilantro, and onion powder. 2. Then stir in the coconut cream and place the vegetables in the Crisper Tray. Slide the Crisper Tray into shelf position 4/5. Select the Vegetables setting. Set the temperature to 360°F and the time to 8 minutes. Press Start/Pause to begin cooking. Flip them halfway through the cooking time. 3. Top with Cheddar cheese and serve.

Chili Kabocha Squash

Prep Time: 10 minutes | Cook Time: 12 minutes | Servings: 4

10 oz. Kabocha squash

1 teaspoon onion powder

1 oz. scallions, chopped

1 tablespoon olive oil

½ teaspoon chili flakes

1. Cut the squash into cubes and sprinkle with olive oil, onion powder, and chili flakes. 2. Put the kabocha squash the Crisper Tray. Slide the Crisper Tray into shelf position 4/5. Select the Airfry setting. Set the temperature to 365°F and the time to 12 minutes. Press Start/Pause to begin cooking. Flip them halfway through the cooking time. 3. Garnish with scallions and serve.

Nutty Cauliflower and Prosciutto Mix

Prep Time: 5 minutes | Cook Time: 25 minutes | Servings: 4

1-pound cauliflower, chopped

2 oz. spring onions, chopped

½ teaspoon white pepper

4 oz. prosciutto, chopped

1 pecan, chopped

3 tablespoons apple cider vinegar

1 tablespoon avocado oil

1. Place all ingredients in the crisper tray and mix well. 2. Slide the Crisper Tray into shelf position 4/5. Select the Vegetables setting. Set the temperature to 360°F and the time to 25 minutes. Press Start/Pause to begin cooking. Flip them halfway through the cooking time.

Jarlsberg Cheese Roasted Cauliflower & Broccoli

Prep Time: 10 minutes | Cook Time: 15 minutes | Servings: 4

10 oz. broccoli, chopped

10 oz. cauliflower, chopped

4 oz. Jarlsberg cheese, grated

2 tablespoons apple cider vinegar

1 tablespoon avocado oil

1. In a large bowl, combine the broccoli, cauliflower, avocado oil and apple cider vinegar. 2. Put the vegetables in the crisper tray and top with Jarlsberg cheese. 3. Slide the Crisper Tray into shelf position 4/5. Select the Vegetables setting. Set the temperature to 365°F and the time to 15 minutes. Press Start/Pause to begin cooking. Serve warm.

Delicious Parmesan Zucchini Noodles

Prep Time: 20 minutes | Cook Time: 5 minutes | Servings: 4

3 zucchinis, trimmed

1 tablespoon coconut oil

1 oz. Parmesan, grated

1. Use a spiralizer to spiralize the zucchini, then mix with the coconut oil and Parmesan cheese. 2. Place the mixture in the crisper tray. Slide the Crisper Tray into shelf position 4/5. Select the Vegetables setting. Set the temperature to 360°F and the time to 5 minutes. Press Start/Pause to begin cooking. 3. Carefully mix the cooked noodles and serve warm.

Hot Lemony Cauliflower

Prep Time: 5 minutes | Cook Time: 14 minutes | Servings: 4

1-pound cauliflower florets

2 tablespoons sesame oil

2 tablespoons keto hot sauce

3 tablespoons lemon juice

½ teaspoon white pepper

1. In a small bowl, mix up the sesame oil, hot sauce, lemon juice, and white pepper. 2. Then mix cauliflower florets with the lemon juice mixture and place in the Crisper Tray. Slide the Crisper Tray into shelf position 4/5. Select the Vegetables setting. Set the temperature to 360°F and the time to 14 minutes. Press Start/Pause to begin cooking. Flip them halfway through the cooking time.

Herbed Garlicky Broccoli Steaks

Prep Time: 5 minutes | Cook Time: 12 minutes | Servings: 4

2-pound broccoli head

1 tablespoon coconut oil, melted

1 teaspoon garlic powder

½ teaspoon dried oregano

1. Cut the broccoli head into steaks and rub them with coconut oil, dried oregano and garlic powder. 2. Put the broccoli steaks in the crisper tray. Slide the Crisper Tray into shelf position 4/5. Select the Airfry setting. Set the temperature to 365°F and the time to 12 minutes. Press Start/Pause to begin cooking. Flip them halfway through the cooking time.

Aromatic Broccoli with Scallions

Prep Time: 5 minutes | Cook Time: 15 minutes | Servings: 4

1-pound broccoli, roughly chopped

1 tablespoon olive oil

1 teaspoon salt

2 oz. scallions, chopped

1. Place the broccoli in a bowl and toss with olive oil and salt. 2. Then transfer the broccoli to the Crisper Tray. Slide the Crisper Tray into shelf position 4/5. Select the Vegetables setting. Set the temperature to 365°F and the time to 10 minutes. Press Start/Pause to begin cooking. Flip them halfway through the cooking time. 3. Sprinkle with scallions and cook for 5 minutes more.

Parmesan Eggplant Mash

Prep Time: 10 minutes | Cook Time: 20 minutes | Servings: 6

12 oz. eggplants, peeled

1 tablespoon coconut oil

1 garlic clove, minced

1 oz. Parmesan, grated

1 tablespoon cream cheese

1. Chop the eggplants and sprinkle with coconut oil. 2. Place the eggplants in the Crisper Tray. Slide the Crisper Tray into shelf position 4/5. Select the Vegetables setting. Set the temperature to 350°F and the time to 20 minutes. Press Start/Pause to begin cooking. 3. Transfer the cooked eggplants to a blender. 4. Add all of the remaining ingredients and blend the mixture until smooth.

Coconut Jicama Fries

Prep Time: 15 minutes | Cook Time: 7 minutes | Servings: 5

15 oz. jicama, peeled, cut into sticks

1 egg, beaten

¼ cup heavy cream

½ cup coconut shred

1 teaspoon chili powder

Cooking spray

1. In a small shallow bowl, whisk the egg with heavy cream and chili powder. 2. Dip the jicama sticks in the egg mixture and then coat in the coconut shred. 3. Put the coated jicama in the Crisper Tray and spray with cooking spray. 4. Slide the Crisper Tray into shelf position 4/5. Select the Airfry setting. Set the temperature to 390°F and the time to 7 minutes. Press Start/Pause to begin cooking. Serve warm.

Chapter 3 Poultry

Crisp Parmesan Chicken with Marinara Sauce

Prep Time: 20 minutes | Cook Time: 18 minutes | Servings: 2

¾ cup panko bread crumbs

2 tablespoons extra-virgin olive oil

¼ cup grated Parmesan cheese

1 large egg

1 tablespoon all-purpose flour

¾ teaspoon garlic powder

½ teaspoon dried oregano

Salt and pepper

2 (8-ounce) boneless, skinless chicken breasts, trimmed

2 ounces whole-milk mozzarella cheese, shredded (½ cup)

¼ cup jarred marinara sauce, warmed

2 tablespoons chopped fresh basil

1. In a bowl, toss the panko with olive oil until evenly coated. Microwave, stirring often, until light golden brown, about 1 to 3 minutes. Then transfer to shallow bowl and allow it to cool slightly; stir in Parmesan. 2. In another shallow bowl, whisk together the egg, flour, oregano, ⅛ teaspoon salt, garlic powder, and ⅛ teaspoon pepper. 3. Pound chicken to an even thickness as desired. Pat dry with paper towels and season with salt and black pepper. Take 1 chicken breast at a time, dip in the egg mixture and let excess drip off, then coat with the panko mixture and press gently to adhere. 4. Lightly spray the crisper tray with vegetable oil spray. Arrange breasts in the Crisper Tray. Slide the Crisper Tray into shelf position 4/5. Select the Airfry setting. Set the temperature to 400°F and the time to 14 minutes. Press Start/Pause to begin cooking. Flip them halfway through the cooking time. Cook until chicken is crisp. 5. Sprinkle the chicken with mozzarella and cook for 1 more minute. Transfer chicken to serving plates. Place 2 tablespoons of marinara sauce on each chicken breast and sprinkle with basil. Serve warm.

Greek Cheese Chicken-Spinach Meatballs

Prep Time: 10 minutes | Cook Time: 12 minutes | Servings: 1

½ oz. finely ground pork rinds

1 lb. ground chicken

1 tsp. Greek seasoning

⅓ cup feta, crumbled

⅓ cup frozen spinach, drained and thawed

1. In a large bowl, combine all the ingredients with your hands. Shape this mixture into 2-inch balls. 2. Place the balls in the Crisper Tray. Slide the Crisper Tray into shelf position 4/5. Select the Airfry setting. Set the temperature to 350°F and the time to 12 minutes. Press Start/Pause to begin cooking. Flip them halfway through the cooking time. Cook in batches if necessary. 3. Ensure the internal temperature reaches165°F. Serve with Tzatziki if desired.

Spicy Almond-Crusted Chicken Breasts

Prep Time: 10 minutes | Cook Time: 14 minutes | Servings: 2

½ cup slivered almonds, chopped fine

½ cup panko bread crumbs

2 tablespoons unsalted butter, melted

1 teaspoon grated lemon zest, plus lemon wedges for serving

Salt and pepper

1 large egg

1 tablespoon all-purpose flour

1 teaspoon minced fresh thyme or ½ teaspoon dried

Pinch cayenne pepper

2 (8-ounce) boneless, skinless chicken breasts, trimmed

1. In a microwave-safe bowl, combine almonds, melted butter, panko, lemon zest, and ¼ teaspoon salt and microwave, stirring occasionally, until the panko is light golden brown and the almonds are fragrant, about 4 minutes. Transfer to shallow bowl and set aside to cool. In a second shallow bowl, whisk together the egg, thyme, flour, and cayenne. 2. Pound the chicken to uniform thickness as needed and pat dry with paper towels. Then season with salt and black pepper. Working with 1 breast at a time, dredge in egg mixture and drip off any excess, then coat with the panko mixture, pressing gently to adhere. 3. Lightly spray the crisper tray with vegetable oil spray. Place breasts in the tray, spaced evenly apart. Slide the Crisper Tray into shelf position 4/5. Select the Airfry setting. Set the temperature to 400°F and the time to 14 minutes. Press Start/Pause to begin cooking. Flip them halfway through the cooking time. 4. Serve with lemon wedges.

Italian Seasoned Chicken with Tomatoes & Zucchinis

Prep Time: 5 minutes | Cook Time: 25 minutes | Servings: 4

4 chicken breasts, skinless, boneless and halved

2 zucchinis, sliced

4 tomatoes, cut into wedges

2 yellow bell peppers, cut into wedges

2 tablespoons olive oil

1 teaspoon Italian seasoning

1. Combine all the ingredients in the baking pan and toss well. 2. Slide the baking pan into shelf position 4/5. Select the Airfry setting. Set the temperature to 380°F and the time to 25 minutes. Press Start/Pause to begin cooking. 3. Divide everything between plates and serve.

Crispy Hazelnut-Crusted Chicken Tenders

Prep Time: 10 minutes | Cook Time: 10 minutes | Servings: 4

1-pound chicken fillet

3 oz. hazelnuts, grinded

2 egg whites, whisked

½ teaspoon ground black pepper

½ teaspoon salt

1 tablespoon coconut flour

1 teaspoon avocado oil

1. Cut the chicken into 4 tenders and sprinkle them with salt and pepper. 2. In a bowl, mix together the grinded hazelnuts and coconut flour. 3. Dip the chicken tenders in the whisked egg and coat in the hazelnut mixture. 4. Place the chicken tenders in the crisper tray and spray with avocado oil. 5. Slide the Crisper Tray into shelf position 4/5. Select the Chicken setting. Set the temperature to 365°F and the time to 10 minutes. Press Start/Pause to begin cooking. Flip them halfway through the cooking time.

Herbed Chicken Breasts and Green Beans

Prep Time: 5 minutes | Cook Time: 35 minutes | Servings: 4

4 chicken breasts, skinless, boneless and halved

10 ounces chicken stock

1 teaspoon oregano, dried

10 ounces green beans, trimmed and

halved

2 tablespoons olive oil

A pinch of salt and black pepper

1 tablespoon parsley, chopped

1. Heat a pan that fits the air fryer with oil over medium-high heat, add the chicken and cook for 2 minutes per side. Add the remaining ingredients and toss until well combined. 2. Slide the wire rack into shelf position 4/5. Place the pan on the wire rack. Select the Chicken setting. Set the temperature to 380°F and the time to 30 minutes. Press Start/Pause to begin cooking. 3. Divide everything between plates and serve.

Lemongrass Hens

Prep Time: 20 minutes | Cook Time: 65 minutes | Servings: 4

14 oz. hen (chicken)

1 teaspoon lemongrass

1 teaspoon ground coriander

1 oz. celery stalk, chopped

1 teaspoon dried cilantro

3 spring onions, diced

2 tablespoons avocado oil

2 tablespoons lime juice

½ teaspoon lemon zest, grated

1 teaspoon salt

1 tablespoon apple cider vinegar

1 teaspoon chili powder

½ teaspoon ground black pepper

1. In a bowl, mix together the lemongrass, dried cilantro, lime juice, lemon zest, ground coriander, salt, apple cider vinegar, and black pepper. 2. Add the spring onions and celery stalk. Stir everything until well combined. Rub the hen with the spice mixture and let rest for 10 minutes to marinate. 3. Then place the hen in the crisper tray. Slide the Crisper Tray into shelf position 4/5. Select the Chicken setting. Set the temperature to 375°F and the time to 55 minutes. Press Start/Pause to begin cooking. 4. Flip them and cook for 10 minutes longer.

Roasted Pecan-Crusted Chicken Thighs

Prep Time: 10 minutes | Cook Time: 22 minutes | Servings: 1

1 lb. chicken thighs

Salt and pepper

2 cups roasted pecans

1 cup water

1 cup flour

1. Season the chicken with salt and pepper, set aside. 2. In a food processor, pulse the roasted pecans into a flour-like consistency. 3. Fill a bowl with the water. In a second bowl, add the flour, and a third with the pecans. 4. Coat the chicken thighs in the flour. Mix the remaining flour with the processed pecans. 5. Dredge the thighs in the water and then press into the flour-pecan mix, ensuring the chicken is well coated. 6. Arrange the chicken thighs in the crisper tray. Slide the Crisper Tray into shelf position 4/5. Select the Chicken setting. Set the temperature to 400°F and the time to 22 minutes. Press Start/Pause to begin cooking. Flip them halfway through the cooking time. You can cook for an additional 5 minutes if you would like a darker-brown color of the chicken. Serve warm.

Spicy Chicken Breasts with Parsley

Prep Time: 5 minutes | Cook Time: 20 minutes | Servings: 4

4 chicken breasts, skinless and boneless

1 teaspoon chili powder

A pinch of salt and black pepper

A drizzle of olive oil

1 teaspoon smoked paprika

1 teaspoon garlic powder

1 tablespoon parsley, chopped

1. Season chicken with salt and black pepper. 2. In a small bowl, mix up the rest of ingredients except the parsley. 3. Rub the chicken breasts with the spice mixture and place in the crisper tray. 4. Slide the Crisper Tray into shelf position 4/5. Select the Chicken setting. Set the temperature to 350°F and the time to 20 minutes. Press Start/Pause to begin cooking. Flip them halfway through the cooking time. 5. Divide between plates, sprinkle with the parsley and serve.

Herbed Chicken Thighs & Okra

Prep Time: 5 minutes | Cook Time: 30 minutes | Servings: 4

4 chicken thighs, bone-in and skinless

A pinch of salt and black pepper

1 cup okra

½ cup butter, melted

Zest of 1 lemon, grated

4 garlic cloves, minced

1 tablespoon thyme, chopped

1 tablespoon parsley, chopped

1. Heat a pan suitable for an air fryer over medium heat, add half the butter and cook the chicken legs for 2-3 minutes on both sides. Add the rest of the butter, okra and all the remaining ingredients and stir. 2. Slide the wire rack into shelf position 4/5. Place the pan on the wire rack. Select the Chicken setting. Set the temperature to 370°F and the time to 20 minutes. Press Start/Pause to begin cooking. 3. Divide between plates and serve.

Lemon-Chili Chicken Drumsticks

Prep Time: 10 minutes | Cook Time: 20 minutes | Servings: 6

6 chicken drumsticks

1 teaspoon dried oregano

1 tablespoon lemon juice

½ teaspoon lemon zest, grated

1 teaspoon ground cumin

½ teaspoon chili flakes

1 teaspoon garlic powder

½ teaspoon ground coriander

1 tablespoon avocado oil

1. Rub the chicken drumsticks with oregano, lemon juice, lemon zest, garlic powder, cumin, chili flakes, and ground coriander. 2. Then sprinkle them with avocado oil and place in the crisper tray. Slide the Crisper Tray into shelf position 4/5. Select the Chicken setting. Set the temperature to 375°F and the time to 20 minutes. Press Start/Pause to begin cooking. Serve warm.

Garlicky Lemon Chicken Wings

Prep Time: 5 minutes | Cook Time: 30 minutes | Servings: 4

2 pounds chicken wings

¼ cup olive oil

Juice of 2 lemons

Zest of 1 lemon, grated

A pinch of salt and black pepper

2 garlic cloves, minced

1. In a bowl, toss the chicken wings with the remaining ingredients until well coated. 2. Place the chicken wings in the Crisper Tray. Slide the Crisper Tray into shelf position 4/5 and slide the Baking Pan into shelf position 6 to catch the drippings. Select the Wings setting. Set the temperature to 400°F and the time to 30 minutes. Press Start/Pause to begin cooking. Flip them halfway through the cooking time. 3. Divide between plates and serve with salad.

Coconut Cheese Chicken Meatballs

Prep Time: 10 minutes | Cook Time: 12 minutes | Servings: 6

12 oz. ground chicken

½ cup coconut flour

2 egg whites, whisked

1 teaspoon ground black pepper

1 egg yolk

1 teaspoon salt

4 oz. Provolone cheese, grated

1 teaspoon ground oregano

½ teaspoon chili powder

1 tablespoon avocado oil

1. In a large bowl, mix up the ground chicken, egg yolk, black pepper, salt, Provolone cheese, oregano, and chili powder. 2. Stir the mixture until homogenous and shape them into the small meatballs. Dip the meatballs in the whisked egg whites and dredge in the coconut flour. 3. Place the chicken meatballs in the crisper tray. Slide the Crisper Tray into shelf position 4/5. Select the Airfry setting. Set the temperature to 370°F and the time to 12 minutes. Press Start/Pause to begin cooking. Flip them halfway through the cooking time.

Teriyaki Chicken Wings

Prep Time: 10 minutes | Cook Time: 25 minutes | Servings: 4

¼ tsp. ground ginger

2 tsp. minced garlic

½ cup sugar-free teriyaki sauce

2 lb. chicken wings

2 tsp. baking powder

1. In a small bowl, mix together the garlic, ginger, and teriyaki sauce. Place the chicken wings in a large bowl and pour the mixture over them. Toss until the chicken is well coated. 2. Refrigerate for at least one hour. 3. Remove the marinated chicken wings from the fridge and add the baking powder, tossing to coat well. Then place the chicken in the crisper tray. 4. Slide the Crisper Tray into shelf position 4/5 and slide the Baking Pan into shelf position 6 to catch the drippings. Select the Wings setting. Set the temperature to 400°F and the time to 25 minutes. Press Start/Pause to begin cooking. Flip them halfway through the cooking time. 5. The internal temperature should be reached 165°F, then remove from the air fryer and serve immediately.

Buffalo Cheese Chicken Slices

Prep Time: 10 minutes | Cook Time: 8 minutes | Servings: 4

1 egg

1 cup mozzarella cheese, shredded

¼ cup buffalo sauce

1 cup cooked chicken, shredded

¼ cup feta cheese

1. In a medium bowl, combine all ingredients except for the feta. Line the crisper tray with parchment paper. Lay the mixture into the tray and press it into a circle about ½-inch thick. Crumble the feta cheese over it. 2. Slide the Crisper Tray into shelf position 4/5. Select the Airfry setting. Set the temperature to 400°F and the time to 8 minutes. Press Start/Pause to begin cooking. 3. Let rest for a few minutes in the air fryer and cut the mixture into slices. Serve hot.

Crispy Spicy Chicken Strips

Prep Time: 10 minutes | Cook Time: 20 minutes | Servings: 1

¼ cup hot sauce

1 lb. boneless skinless chicken tenders

1 tsp. garlic powder

1½ oz. pork rinds, finely ground

1 tsp chili powder

1. In a bowl, toss the chicken tenders with hot sauce until the chicken is completely coated. 2. In another bowl, mix up the ground pork rinds, garlic powder, and chili powder. Dredge the chicken tenders in this mixture. 3. Place the coated chicken tenders in the crisper tray. Slide the Crisper Tray into shelf position 4/5. Select the Airfry setting. Set the temperature to 375°F and the time to 20 minutes. Press Start/Pause to begin cooking. 4. Serve warm with your favorite dips and sides.

Flavorful Italian Chicken Thighs

Prep Time: 10 minutes | Cook Time: 20 minutes | Servings: 4

4 skin-on bone-in chicken thighs

2 tbsp. unsalted butter, melted

3 tsp. Italian herbs

½ tsp. garlic powder

¼ tsp. onion powder

1. Brush the chicken thighs with melted butter. 2. In a small bowl, mix up the herbs, garlic powder and onion powder, then massage into the chicken thighs. Place the chicken thighs in the crisper tray. 3. Slide the Crisper Tray into shelf position 4/5. Select the Chicken setting. Set the temperature to 380°F and the time to 20 minutes. Press Start/Pause to begin cooking. Flip them halfway through the cooking time. 4. The internal temperature should be reached 165°F, then remove from the fryer and serve.

Chicken Pizza Crusts

Prep Time: 10 minutes | Cook Time: 30 minutes | Servings: 1

½ cup mozzarella, shredded

¼ cup parmesan cheese, grated

1 lb. ground chicken

1. In a big bowl, mix together all the ingredients and then spread the mixture out and divide into four equal sized portions. 2. Cut a piece of parchment paper into four circles about six inches in diameter, then place some of the chicken mixture in the center of each circle, flattening the mixture to fill the circles. 3. Arrange the circles in the crisper tray in one layer. Slide the Crisper Tray into shelf position 4/5. Select the Airfry setting. Set the temperature to 375°F and the time to 25 minutes. Press Start/Pause to begin cooking. Flip them halfway through the cooking time. 4. Once done cooking, top with cheese and the toppings of your choice. Cook the topped crusts for 5 more minutes if desired. 5. Serve hot, or freeze and save for later!

Turkey Breast with Mashed Strawberry

Prep Time: 10 minutes | Cook Time: 37 minutes | Servings: 2

2 lb. turkey breast

1 tbsp. olive oil

Salt and pepper

1 cup fresh strawberries

1. Place the turkey breast in a bowl and massage with olive oil, then season with salt and pepper. 2. Place the turkey breast in the crisper tray. Slide the Crisper Tray into shelf position 4/5. Select the Airfry setting. Set the temperature to 375°F and the time to 30 minutes. Press Start/Pause to begin cooking. Flip them halfway through the cooking time. 3. Meanwhile, blend the strawberries in a food processor until smooth. 4. Heap the strawberries over the cooked turkey and cook for a final 7 minutes. Enjoy.

Palatable Pesto Chicken Legs

Prep Time: 10 minutes | Cook Time: 25 minutes | Servings: 4

12 oz. chicken legs

1 teaspoon sesame oil

½ teaspoon chili flakes

4 teaspoons pesto sauce

1. In the shallow bowl, mix together the pesto sauce, chili flakes, and sesame oil. Rub the chicken legs with the pesto mixture. 2. Place the chicken legs in the Crisper Tray. Slide the Crisper Tray into shelf position 4/5. Select the Chicken setting. Set the temperature to 390°F and the time to 25 minutes. Press Start/Pause to begin cooking. Serve hot.

Sugar-Free Cheese Chicken & Pepperoni Pizza

Prep Time: 10 minutes | Cook Time: 15 minutes | Servings: 6

2 cups cooked chicken, cubed

20 slices pepperoni

1 cup sugar-free pizza sauce

1 cup mozzarella cheese, shredded

¼ cup parmesan cheese, grated

1. Place the chicken, pepperoni and pizza sauce in the baking pan. Toss until the meat is well coated with the sauce. 2. Top with the parmesan and mozzarella. 3. Slide the baking pan into shelf position 4/5. Select the Airfry setting. Set the temperature to 375°F and the time to 15 minutes. Press Start/Pause to begin cooking. 4. Serve hot.

Crunchy Chicken Nuggets

Prep Time: 25 minutes | Cook Time: 20 minutes | Servings: 4

4 (8-ounce) boneless, skinless chicken breasts, trimmed

Salt and pepper

3 tablespoons sugar

3 cups panko bread crumbs

¼ cup extra-virgin olive oil

3 large eggs

3 tablespoons all-purpose flour

1 tablespoon onion powder

¾ teaspoon garlic powder

1. Pound chicken to even thickness as needed. Cut each breast diagonally into thirds, then cut each piece into thirds. In a large container with 2 quarts of cold water, dissolve 3 tablespoons salt and sugar. Add chicken, cover, and let rest for 15 minutes. 2. Meanwhile, in a bowl, toss the panko with oil until evenly coated. Microwave, stirring often, until light golden brown, about 5 minutes. Then transfer to shallow bowl and let cool slightly. In another shallow bowl, whisk together the eggs, onion powder, flour, garlic powder, 1 teaspoon salt, and ¼ teaspoon pepper. 3. Set a wire rack in rimmed baking sheet. Remove chicken from the brine and pat dry with paper towels. 4. Working with chicken a few pieces at a time, dip in egg mixture and allow excess to drip off, then coat with the panko mixture, pressing gently to make it stick; transfer chicken to the prepared rack. Freeze until firm, about 4 hours. (Frozen chicken pieces can be stored in a zipper bag in the freezer for up to 1 month). 5. Lightly spray the crisper tray with vegetable oil spray. Place up to 18 nuggets in the tray. Slide the Crisper Tray into shelf position 4/5. Select the Airfry setting. Set the temperature to 400°F and the time to 6 minutes. Press Start/Pause to begin cooking. 6. Transfer the chicken nuggets to clean bowl and gently toss to redistribute. 7. Return nuggets to the air fryer and cook until chicken is crisp and registers 160°F, 6 to 10 minutes. Serve with the sauce to your liking

Spicy Chicken Jalapeño Sandwich

Prep Time: 20 minutes | Cook Time: 14 minutes | Servings: 4

1 cup panko bread crumbs

2 tablespoons extra-virgin olive oil

1 large egg

3 tablespoons hot sauce

1 tablespoon all-purpose flour

½ teaspoon garlic powder

Salt and pepper

2 (8-ounce) boneless, skinless chicken breasts, trimmed

¼ cup mayonnaise

4 hamburger buns, toasted if desired

2 cups shredded iceberg lettuce

¼ cup jarred sliced jalapeños

1. In a bowl, toss the panko with oil until evenly coated. Microwave, stirring often, until light golden brown, 1 to 3 minutes. Transfer to shallow bowl and set aside to cool. In a shallow bowl, whisk together the egg, flour, garlic powder, 2 tablespoons hot sauce, ⅛ teaspoon salt, and ⅛ teaspoon pepper. 2. Pound chicken to an even thickness as desired. Cut each chicken breast in half horizontally, pat dry with paper towels, and season with salt and black pepper. Taking one piece of chicken at a time, dip it in the egg mixture, letting the excess drip off, then coat it in the panko mixture and press gently to make it stick to the chicken. 3. Lightly spray the crisper tray with vegetable oil spray. Place the coated chicken breasts in the tray. Slide the Crisper Tray into shelf position 4/5. Select the Airfry setting. Set the temperature to 400°F and the time to 14 minutes. Press Start/Pause to begin cooking. Flip them halfway through the cooking time. 4. In a small bowl, mix up the mayonnaise and remaining 1 tablespoon hot sauce. Spread the mayonnaise mixture evenly over the bun bottoms, then top with 1 piece of chicken, lettuce, jalapeños, and bun tops. Serve..

Chapter 4 Beef, Pork, and Lamb

Cheese Pepperoni Bread Pockets

Prep Time: 10 minutes | Cook Time: 10 minutes | Servings: 4

4 bread slices, 1-inch thick

olive oil for misting

24 slices pepperoni (about 2 ounces)

1 ounce roasted red peppers, drained and

patted dry

1 ounce Pepper Jack cheese cut into 4 slices

Pizza sauce (optional)

1. Spray both sides of the bread with olive oil. 2. Stand the bread slices upright and cut a deep slit in the top to create a pocket—almost to the bottom crust but not all the way through. 3. Stuff each bread pocket with 6 slices of pepperoni, a strip of roasted red pepper, and a slice of cheese. 4. Place the bread pockets in the crisper tray, standing up. Slide the Crisper Tray into shelf position 4/5. Select the Airfry setting. Set the temperature to 360°F and the time to 10 minutes. Press Start/Pause to begin cooking. 5. Serve hot with pizza sauce.

Pizza Tortilla Rolls

Prep Time: 10 minutes | Cook Time: 22 minutes | Servings: 4

1 teaspoon butter

½ medium onion, slivered

½ red or green bell pepper, julienned

4 ounces fresh white mushrooms, chopped

8 flour tortillas (6- or 7-inch size)

½ cup pizza sauce

8 thin slices deli ham

24 pepperoni slices (about 1½ ounces)

1 cup (about 4 ounces) shredded mozzarella cheese

Oil for misting or cooking spray

1. Combine the onions, butter, bell pepper, and mushrooms in the baking pan. Slide the baking pan into shelf position 4/5. Select the Vegetables setting. Set the temperature to 390°F and the time to 3 minutes. Press Start/Pause to begin cooking. Stir and cook for an additional 3 to 4 minutes until just crisp and tender. Remove the baking pan from the air fryer and set aside. 2. To assemble the rolls, spread 2 teaspoons of pizza sauce on one half of each tortilla. Top with a slice of ham and 3 slices of pepperoni. Divide the cooked vegetables among the tortillas and top with cheese. 3. Roll up tortillas, secure with toothpicks if necessary, and spray with oil. 4. Arrange 4 rolls in the crisper tray. Slide the Crisper Tray into shelf position 4/5. Select the Airfry setting. Set the temperature to 390°F and the time to 8 minutes. Press Start/Pause to begin cooking. Flip them halfway through the cooking time. 5. Repeat the same steps to cook the remaining pizza rolls.

Tasty BBQ Beef Steaks

Prep Time: 15 minutes | Cook Time: 15 minutes | Servings: 4

4 beef steaks

1 cup keto BBQ sauce

1 tablespoon olive oil

1. Mix together the olive oil with BBQ sauce in a shallow bowl. 2. Slide the Wire Rack into shelf position 2. Mix beef steaks with sauce mixture and place on the wire rack. Spray the steaks with olive oil. 3. Select the Steak setting. Set the temperature to 400°F and the time to 15 minutes. Serve and enjoy!

Coconut Beef Steak

Prep Time: 10 minutes | Cook Time: 16 minutes | Servings: 4

2-pounds beef steak

3 tablespoons coconut oil

1 teaspoon coconut shred

1 teaspoon dried basil

1. Rub the beef steak with dried basil and coconut shred. 2. Slide the Wire Rack into shelf position 2. Then brush the beef steak with coconut oil and place it on the wire rack. 3. Select the Steak setting. Set the temperature to 390°F and the time to 16 minutes. Halfway through the cooking time, flip the steaks.

Steak Fingers

Prep Time: 10 minutes | Cook Time: 10 minutes | Servings: 4

4 small beef cube steaks

Salt and pepper

½ cup flour

Oil for misting or cooking spray

1. Cut cube steaks into 1-inch wide strips. 2. Season lightly with salt and pepper. 3. Roll in flour to coat all sides. 4. Spray air fryer basket with cooking spray or oil. 5. Place steak strips in a single layer in the crisper tray, close to but not touching. Spray top of steak strips with oil or cooking spray. 6. Air fry at 390°F for 4 minutes, flip the strips over and spray with oil or cooking spray. 7. Cook for 4 more minutes and test with fork for doneness. 8. Cook for an additional 2 to 4 minutes or until well done if needed.

Meat & Vegetables Egg Rolls

Prep Time: 25 minutes | Cook Time: 15 minutes | Servings: 8

¼ pound very lean ground beef

¼ pound lean ground pork

1 tablespoon soy sauce

1 teaspoon olive oil

½ cup grated carrots

2 green onions, chopped

2 cups grated Napa cabbage

¼ cup chopped water chestnuts

¼ teaspoon salt

¼ teaspoon garlic powder

¼ teaspoon black pepper

1 egg

1 tablespoon water

8 egg roll wraps

Oil for misting or cooking spray

1. In a large skillet, brown the beef and pork with soy sauce. Transfer the cooked meat to a bowl, drain, and set aside. 2. Clean and drain the skillet. Add olive oil, onions and carrots. Sauté until the carrots are tender, about 1 minute. 3. Stir in cabbage, cover, and cook for 1 minute or until the cabbage is slightly wilts. Remove from the heat. 4. In a big bowl, combine the cooked meats and vegetables, water chestnuts, garlic powder, salt, and pepper. Stir to mix well. 5. In a small bowl, whisk together egg and water. 6. Fill each egg roll wrapper with equal amount of filling. Roll up and brush all over with egg wash to seal. Lightly spray with olive oil. 7. Arrange the egg rolls in the crisper tray. Slide the Crisper Tray into shelf position 4/5. Select the Airfry setting. Set the temperature to 390°F and the time to 8 minutes. Press Start/Pause to begin cooking. Flip them halfway through the cooking time. Cook until golden brown and crispy.

Aromatic Lamb Steak

Prep Time: 10 minutes | Cook Time: 12 minutes | Servings: 2

14 oz. lamb steak

1 teaspoon ground coriander

1 teaspoon garlic powder

1 tablespoon olive oil

1. Rub the lamb steak with garlic powder, ground coriander, and olive oil. 2. Slide the Wire Rack into shelf position 2 with the Baking Pan placed underneath. 3. Then place the lamb steak on the wire rack. 4. Select the Steak setting. Set the temperature to 385°F and the time to 12 minutes. Halfway through the cooking time, flip the steaks.

Easy Air Fried Pork Chops

Prep Time: 10 minutes | Cook Time: 18 minutes | Servings: 2

2 bone-in, center cut pork chops, 1-inch thick (10 ounces each)

2 teaspoons Worcestershire sauce

Salt and pepper

Cooking spray

1. Rub both sides of pork chops with Worcestershire sauce. 2. Season with salt and black pepper. 3. Spray the crisper tray with cooking spray and place the chops inside. Slide the Crisper Tray into shelf position 4/5. Select the Airfry setting. Set the temperature to 360°F and the time to 18 minutes. Press Start/Pause to begin cooking. 4. Let rest for 5 minutes before serving.

Sesame Pork Cutlets with Aloha Salsa

Prep Time: 10 minutes | Cook Time: 8 minutes | Servings: 4

2 eggs

2 tablespoons milk

¼ cup flour

¼ cup panko breadcrumbs

4 teaspoons sesame seeds

1 pound boneless, thin pork cutlets (⅜- to ½-inch thick)

Lemon pepper and salt

¼ cup cornstarch

Oil for misting or cooking spray

Aloha Salsa:

1 cup fresh pineapple, chopped in small pieces

¼ cup red onion, finely chopped

¼ cup green or red bell pepper, chopped

½ teaspoon ground cinnamon

1 teaspoon low-sodium soy sauce

⅛ teaspoon crushed red pepper

⅛ teaspoon ground black pepper

1. In a medium bowl, mix together all ingredients for salsa. Cover and refrigerate while cooking the pork. 2. In a shallow bowl, whisk together the eggs and milk. 3. In another shallow bowl, mix together the flour, sesame seeds and panko. 4. Season the pork cutlets with salt and lemon pepper. 5. Dip pork cutlets in cornstarch, then the egg mixture, and finally the panko coating. Spray both sides of the pork cutlets with oil or cooking spray. 6. Arrange the pork cutlets in the crisper tray. Slide the Crisper Tray into shelf position 4/5. Select the Airfry setting. Set the temperature to 390°F and the time to 3 minutes. Press Start/Pause to begin cooking. 7. Then flip the cutlets and spray both sides with oil again, and continue cooking for 4 to 6 minutes. 8. Serve the pork cutlets with salsa on the side.

Spicy Rib Eye Steaks

Prep Time: 10 minutes | Cook Time: 24 minutes | Servings: 4

3-pound rib-eye steak

1 tablespoon keto tomato paste

1 tablespoon avocado oil

1 teaspoon salt

1 teaspoon cayenne pepper

1. In the shallow bowl, mix up the tomato paste, salt, avocado oil, and cayenne pepper. 2. Slide the Wire Rack into shelf position 2 with the Baking Pan placed underneath. 3. Then rub the beef with tomato mixture and place it on the wire rack. 4. Select the Steak setting. Set the temperature to 380°F and the time to 24 minutes. Halfway through the cooking time, flip the steaks.

Cheese Sausage Calzone

Prep Time: 25 minutes | Cook Time: 20 minutes | Servings: 8

Crust:

2 cups white wheat flour, plus more for kneading and rolling

1 package (¼ ounce) Rapid Rise yeast

1 teaspoon salt

½ teaspoon dried basil

1 cup warm water (115°F to 125°F)

2 teaspoons olive oil

Filling:

¼ pound Italian sausage

½ cup ricotta cheese

4 ounces mozzarella cheese, shredded

¼ cup grated Parmesan cheese

Oil for misting or cooking spray

Marinara sauce for serving

1. Crumble the Italian sausage and place in the baking pan. Air fry at 390°F for 5 minutes. Stir, breaking up, and cook for 3 to 4 minutes or until thoroughly cooked. Take out and set on paper towels to drain. 2. In a large bowl, combine the flour, salt, yeast, and basil. Add the warm water and oil and mix until a soft dough forms. Place the dough on a lightly floured board and knead for 3-4 minutes. Let dough rest for 10 minutes. 3. To make the filling, in a medium bowl, mix together the three cheeses and stir in the cooked sausage. 4. Cut the dough into 8 pieces. 5. Press each piece of dough into a circle about 5 inches in diameter. Place two tablespoons of filling on each round. Fold into half-moon shape, pressing edges together firmly. Make sure edges are sealed securely to prevent filling leakage. Spray both sides with oil or cooking spray. 6. Place 4 calzones in the baking pan and bake at 360°F for 5 minutes. Drizzle with oil and cook for 2 to 3 minutes or until the crust is done and browned. 7. Repeat with the remaining calzones. 8. Serve with marinara sauce on the side for dipping.

Garlicky Beef Steaks

Prep Time: 10 minutes | Cook Time: 14 minutes | Servings: 4

4 beef steaks

1 teaspoon garlic powder

1 tablespoon coconut oil

1. Rub the beef steaks with garlic powder and coconut oil. 2. Slide the Wire Rack into shelf position 2 with the Baking Pan placed underneath. Then place the beef steaks on the wire rack. 3. Select the Steak setting. Set the temperature to 400°F and the time to 14 minutes. Halfway through the cooking time, flip the steaks.

Classic Sloppy Joes

Prep Time: 10 minutes | Cook Time: 20 minutes | Servings: 4

Oil for misting or cooking spray

1 pound very lean ground beef

1 teaspoon onion powder

⅓ cup ketchup

¼ cup water

½ teaspoon celery seed

1 tablespoon lemon juice

1½ teaspoons brown sugar

1¼ teaspoons low-sodium Worcestershire sauce

½ teaspoon salt (optional)

½ teaspoon vinegar

⅛ teaspoon dry mustard

Hamburger or slider buns

1. Spray the baking pan with olive oil or nonstick cooking spray. 2. Break the ground beef into small chunks and pile into the pan. 3. Air fry at 390°F for 5 minutes. Stir well and cook for 3 minutes. Stir and cook 2 to 4 minutes more or until meat is cooked through. 4. Remove meat from air fryer, drain, and cut meat into bite-sized pieces with a knife and fork. 5. Give the baking pan a quick rinse to remove any ground meat. 6. Place all the remaining ingredients except the buns in the pan and mix together. 7. Add meat and stir well. 8. Air fry at 330°F for 5 minutes. Stir and cook for 2 more minutes. 9. Scoop onto buns.

Crisp Venison Backstrap

Prep Time: 15 minutes | Cook Time: 10 minutes | Servings: 4

2 eggs

¼ cup milk

1 cup whole wheat flour

½ teaspoon salt

¼ teaspoon pepper

1-pound venison backstrap, sliced

Salt and pepper

Oil for misting or cooking spray

1. In a shallow bowl, whisk together the eggs and milk. 2. In a separate shallow bowl, mix together the flour, salt, and black pepper. Stir to mix well. 3. Season the venison steaks with additional salt and black pepper. Dip in flour, egg mixture, then in flour again, pressing to coat well. 4. Spray steaks with oil or cooking spray on both sides. 5. Slide the Wire Rack into shelf position 2. Place the steaks on the wire rack in a single layer. Select the Steak setting. Set the temperature to 360°F and the time to 8 minutes. 6. When cooking time is up, flip the steaks and spray with oil. Cook for 2 to 4 minutes more, until coating is crispy brown and meat is done to your liking.

Air Fried Coconut Beef Bread

Prep Time: 10 minutes | Cook Time: 25 minutes | Servings: 4

2-pounds ground beef

1 teaspoon minced garlic

1 tablespoon dried parsley

1 teaspoon ground turmeric

¼ cup coconut flour

1 tablespoon coconut oil, softened

1. In a bowl, combine the ground beef, minced garlic, ground turmeric, dried parsley, and coconut flour. 2. Grease the baking pan with coconut oil from inside. 3. Place the ground beef mixture in the baking pan and flatten gently. 4. Air fry the beef bread at 370°F for 25 minutes. Flip it halfway through the cooking time. Serve warm.

Red Meat, Rice & Tomato Stuffed Bell Peppers

Prep Time: 20 minutes | Cook Time: 25 minutes | Servings: 4

¼ pound lean ground pork

¾ pound lean ground beef

¼ cup onion, minced

1 15-ounce can Red Gold crushed tomatoes

1 teaspoon Worcestershire sauce

1 teaspoon barbeque seasoning

1 teaspoon honey

½ teaspoon dried basil

½ cup cooked brown rice

½ teaspoon garlic powder

½ teaspoon oregano

½ teaspoon salt

2 small bell peppers

1. Combine the beef, pork, and onion in the baking pan and air fry at 360°F for 5 minutes. 2. Stir to break up the chunks and cook 3 more minutes. Continue cooking, stirring every 2 minutes, until meat is thoroughly cooked. Remove from pan and drain. 3. In a small saucepan, combine together the tomatoes, barbeque seasoning, honey, Worcestershire, and basil. Stir to mix well. 4. In a large bowl, combine the cooked meat mixture, rice, oregano, garlic powder, and salt. Add ¼ cup of the seasoned tomatoes. Stir to mix well. 5. Cut the peppers in half and remove stems and seeds. 6. Stuff one-fourth of the meat mixture into each pepper half. 7. Place the peppers in the crisper tray and air fry at 360°F for 10 to 12 minutes, until peppers are crisp tender. 8. Heat remaining tomato sauce. Serve by spooning the warm sauce over the stuffed peppers.

Beef Bites with Cream

Prep Time: 10 minutes | Cook Time: 30 minutes | Servings: 4

2-pound beef fillet

1 tablespoon onion powder

¼ cup heavy cream

½ teaspoon salt

1 teaspoon olive oil

1. Cut the beef fillet into small bites and sprinkle with onion powder and salt. 2. Place the beef bites in the crisper tray and add heavy cream. 3. Slide the Crisper Tray into shelf position 4/5. Select the Airfry setting. Set the temperature to 360°F and the time to 30 minutes. Press Start/Pause to begin cooking. Flip them halfway through the cooking time.

Yogurt Beef Strips

Prep Time: 10 minutes | Cook Time: 35 minutes | Servings: 4

2-pounds beef steak, cut into strips

¼ cup plain yogurt

1 teaspoon lemon juice

1 teaspoon white pepper

½ teaspoon dried oregano

Cooking spray

1. In a shallow bowl, mix together the plain yogurt, white pepper, lemon juice, and dried oregano. 2. Dip the beef strips in the plain yogurt mixture. 3. Spray the crisper tray with cooking spray. 4. Slide the Crisper Tray into shelf position 4/5. Select the Airfry setting. Set the temperature to 360°F and the time to 35 minutes. Press Start/Pause to begin cooking. Serve.

Curried Citrus Pork Loin Roast

Prep Time: 10 minutes | Cook Time: 45 minutes | Servings: 8

1 tablespoon lime juice

1 tablespoon orange marmalade

1 teaspoon coarse brown mustard

1 teaspoon curry powder

1 teaspoon dried lemongrass

2-pound boneless pork loin roast

Salt and pepper

Cooking spray

1. Select the Roast setting. Set the temperature to 360°F and the time to 45 minutes. Let the appliance preheat. 2. In a small bowl, mix together the lime juice, mustard, curry powder, marmalade, and lemongrass. 3. Rub this mixture all over of the pork loin. Season with salt and black pepper. 4. Spray the baking pan with cooking spray and place pork roast inside. 5. When the appliance has preheated, slide the Baking Pan into shelf position 4/5. Cook for 45 minutes. 6. Wrap roast in foil and let rest for 10 minutes before slicing.

Mushroom and Bacon Stuffed Beef Roll

Prep Time: 20 minutes | Cook Time: 40 minutes | Servings: 4

1-pound beef loin

2 oz. mushrooms, chopped

1 teaspoon onion powder

1 oz. bacon, chopped, cooked

½ teaspoon dried dill

1 teaspoon chili powder

1 tablespoon avocado oil

½ teaspoon cream cheese

1. Beat the beef loin with a kitchen hammer to flatten it. 2. In a bowl, toss the mushrooms, bacon, dried dill, with onion powder, chili powder, and cream cheese. 3. Place the mixture over the beef loin and roll it. 4. Secure the beef roll with toothpicks and brush with avocado oil. 5. Place the beef roll in the Crisper Tray. Slide the Crisper Tray into shelf position 4/5. Select the Airfry setting. Set the temperature to 370°F and the time to 40 minutes. Press Start/Pause to begin cooking. Serve warm.

Za'atar Beef Chops

Prep Time: 10 minutes | Cook Time: 11 minutes | Servings: 6

6 beef chops

1 tablespoon coconut oil, melted

1 tablespoon za'atar seasonings

1. Select the Roast setting. Set the temperature to 400°F and the time to 11 minutes. Let the appliance preheat. 2. In a small bowl, mix up the za'atar seasonings with coconut oil. 3. Brush the beef chops with the oil mixture. 4. Spray the baking pan with cooking spray and place the beef chops inside. 5. When the appliance has preheated, slide the Baking Pan into shelf position 4/5. Cook for 11 minutes. Serve warm.

Lamb-Cauliflower Fritters

Prep Time: 15 minutes | Cook Time: 20 minutes | Servings: 8

1 teaspoon onion powder

1 teaspoon garlic powder

½ teaspoon ground coriander

1 teaspoon salt

2-pound lamb, minced

½ cup cauliflower, shredded

Cooking spray

1. Spray the air fryer basket with cooking spray from inside. 2. In a large bowl, mix together the lamb, cauliflower, onion powder, salt, garlic powder and ground coriander. 3. Make equal-sized fritters from the beef mixture and place them in the crisper tray. 4. Slide the Crisper Tray into shelf position 4/5. Select the Airfry setting. Set the temperature to 360°F and the time to 20 minutes. Press Start/Pause to begin cooking. Flip them halfway through the cooking time.

Garlicky Beef and Bell Pepper Bowl

Prep Time: 5 minutes | Cook Time: 30 minutes | Servings: 4

1 cup bell pepper, diced

1-pound ground beef

1 garlic clove, diced

1 teaspoon dried oregano

1 teaspoon coconut oil

1 tablespoon cream cheese

1. Combine all the ingredients in a bowl and mix thoroughly. 2. Then transfer the mixture to the baking pan and air fry at 365°F for 30 minutes, tossing them halfway through the cooking time.

Chapter 5 Fish and Seafood

Parmesan-Crusted Snapper Fillets with Almond Sauce

Prep Time: 20 minutes | Cook Time: 15 minutes | Servings: 4

4 skin-on snapper fillets	¼ cup almonds
Sea salt and ground pepper, to taste	2 garlic cloves, pressed
½ cup parmesan cheese, grated `	1 cup tomato paste
2 tablespoons fresh cilantro, chopped	1 teaspoon dried dill weed
½ cup coconut flour	½ teaspoon salt
2 tablespoon flaxseed meal	¼ teaspoon freshly ground mixed
2 medium-sized eggs	peppercorns
For the Almond Sauce:	¼ cup olive oil

1. Season the fish fillets with sea salt and black pepper. 2. In a shallow dish, combine the parmesan cheese and cilantro. 3. In another shallow dish, whisk the eggs until frothy. 4. In a third dish, combine the coconut flour and flaxseed meal. 5. Coat the fish fillets in the flour, then dip in the egg; finally, coat them with the parmesan mixture. 6. Place the fish fillets in the crisper tray. Slide the Crisper Tray into shelf position 4/5. Select the Airfry setting. Set the temperature to 390°F and the time to 15 minutes. Press Start/Pause to begin cooking. 7. Meanwhile, you can prepare the sauce. chop the almonds in a food processor and add the remaining sauce ingredients except the olive oil. 8. Blitz for 30 seconds; then slowly pour in the olive oil and process until smooth. Serve the sauce with the cooked snapper fillets.

Minty Basil Shrimps

Prep Time: 15 minutes | Cook Time: 4 minutes | Servings: 4

½ tablespoon fresh basil leaves, chopped	1 teaspoon smoked cayenne pepper
1½ pounds shrimp, shelled and deveined	½ teaspoon fresh mint, roughly chopped
1½ tablespoons olive oil	½ teaspoon ginger, freshly grated
3 cloves garlic, minced	1 teaspoon sea salt

1. Combine all the ingredients in a mixing bowl and stir until everything is well combined. Let it rest for about 28 minutes. 2. Then transfer the mixture to the baking pan. Slide the baking pan into shelf position 4/5. Select the Airfry setting. Set the temperature to 395°F and the time to 4 minutes.

Herbed Cod Fillets

Prep Time: 15 minutes | Cook Time: 12 minutes | Servings: 4

4 cod fillets

¼ teaspoon fine sea salt

¼ teaspoon ground black pepper, or more to taste

1 teaspoon cayenne pepper

½ cup non-dairy milk

½ cup fresh Italian parsley, coarsely chopped

1 teaspoon dried basil

½ teaspoon dried oregano

1 Italian pepper, chopped

4 garlic cloves, minced

1. Lightly grease the inside of the baking pan with vegetable oil. 2. Season the cod fillets with salt, black pepper, and cayenne pepper. 3. In a food processor, puree the remaining ingredients. Toss the fish fillets with this mixture and arrange them in the baking pan. 4. Slide the baking pan into shelf position 2. Select the Fish setting. Set the temperature to 380°F and the time to 12 minutes. Press Start/Pause to begin cooking. 5. Cook until the cod flakes easily. Enjoy!

Herbed Honey Halibut Steaks

Prep Time: 10 minutes | Cook Time: 10 minutes | Servings: 4

1-pound halibut steaks

Salt and pepper, to your liking

1 teaspoon dried basil

2 tablespoons honey

¼ cup vegetable oil

2½ tablespoons Worcester sauce

1 tablespoon freshly squeezed lemon juice

2 tablespoons vermouth

1 tablespoon fresh parsley leaves, coarsely chopped

1. Combine all the ingredients in a large mixing bowl. Gently stir until the halibut steaks are evenly coated and place in the baking pan. 2. Slide the baking pan into shelf position 2. Select the Fish setting. Set the temperature to 390°F and the time to 10 minutes. Press Start/Pause to begin cooking. Flip halfway through the cooking time. 3. Check for the doneness and cook for a few more minutes if needed. Bon appétit!

Crisp Parmesan-Crusted Fish Fillets

Prep Time: 10 minutes | Cook Time: 12 minutes | Servings: 4

1 cup parmesan, grated

1 teaspoon garlic powder

½ teaspoon shallot powder

1 egg, well whisked

4 white fish fillets

Salt and ground black pepper, to taste

Fresh Italian parsley, to serve

1. Place the parmesan cheese in a shallow bowl. 2. Mix up the shallot powder, garlic powder, and the beaten egg in another bowl. 3. Season the fish fillets with salt and black pepper. Dip each fillet into the egg mixture. 4. Then, dredge the fillets in the parmesan mixture. 5. Place the coated fish fillets in the crisper tray. 6. Slide the Crisper Tray into shelf position 4/5. Select the Airfry setting. Set the temperature to 370°F and the time to 12 minutes. Press Start/Pause to begin cooking. Flip them halfway through the cooking time. 7. Garnish with fresh parsley and serve!

Italian Lemon Sardines

Prep Time: 30 minutes | Cook Time: 12 minutes | Servings: 4

1½ pounds sardines, cleaned and rinsed

Salt and ground black pepper, to savor

1 tablespoon Italian seasoning mix

1 tablespoon lemon juice

1 tablespoon soy sauce

2 tablespoons olive oil

1. Pat dry the sardines with a kitchen towel. Add salt, Italian seasoning mix, black pepper, soy sauce, lemon juice, and olive oil; marinate them for 30 minutes. 2. Then place the marinated sardines in the baking pan. Slide the baking pan into shelf position 2. Select the Fish setting. Set the temperature to 350°F and the time to 5 minutes. Press Start/Pause to begin cooking. 3. After 5 minutes, increase the temperature to 385°F and cook for 7 to 8 minutes longer. 4. Serve and enjoy!

Aromatic Cheesy Shrimps

Prep Time: 15 minutes | Cook Time: 8 minutes | Servings: 2

½ tablespoon fresh parsley, roughly chopped

1½ tablespoons balsamic vinegar

Sea salt flakes, to taste

1-pound shrimp, deveined

1 tablespoon coconut aminos

1 teaspoon Dijon mustard

½ teaspoon garlic powder

1½ tablespoons olive oil

½ teaspoon smoked cayenne pepper

Salt and ground black peppercorns, to savor

1 cup goat cheese, shredded

1. In a bowl, combine all ingredients except the cheese. 2. Place the mixture in the baking pan. Slide the baking pan into shelf position 4/5. Select the Airfry setting. Set the temperature to 385°F and the time to 7 minutes. 3. When cooking time is up, spread the cheese on top and cook for 1 more minute. Serve and enjoy!

Spicy Tuna Egg Casserole

Prep Time: 15 minutes | Cook Time: 20 minutes | Servings: 4

5 eggs, beaten

½ chili pepper, deveined and finely minced

1½ tablespoons sour cream

⅓ teaspoon dried oregano

½ tablespoon sesame oil

⅓ cup yellow onions, chopped

2 cups canned tuna

½ bell pepper, deveined and chopped

⅓ teaspoon dried basil

Fine sea salt and ground black pepper, to taste

1. In a nonstick skillet over medium heat, warm the sesame oil. Then, stir in the onions and peppers and cook for 4 minutes until they are just fragrant. 2. Stir in the chopped canned tuna and cook until heated through. 3. Lightly grease the baking pan with cooking spray. Add in sautéed tuna/pepper mix. Add the remaining ingredients and gently stir well. 4. Slide the baking pan into shelf position 4/5. Select the Airfry setting. Set the temperature to 325°F and the time to 12 minutes. Press Start/Pause to begin cooking. 5. Garnish with Tabasco sauce if desired. Serve warm.

Parmesan Curried Peppercorn Halibut Fillets

Prep Time: 10 minutes | Cook Time: 10 minutes | Servings: 4

2 medium-sized halibut fillets

1 teaspoon curry powder

½ teaspoon ground coriander

Kosher salt and freshly cracked mixed peppercorns, to taste

1½ tablespoons olive oil

½ cup parmesan cheese, grated

2 eggs

½ teaspoon hot paprika

A few drizzles of tabasco sauce

1. In a shallow bowl, combine the parmesan cheese with olive oil. 2. In a second shallow bowl, whisk in the egg. 3. Drizzle the halibut fillets with Tabasco sauce and toss with hot paprika, coriander, salt, curry, and peppercorns. Mix well. 4. Dip each fish fillet into the egg; then roll it over the parmesan mix. 5. Place the fish fillets in a single layer in the crisper tray. Slide the Crisper Tray into shelf position 4/5. Select the Airfry setting. Set the temperature to 365°F and the time to 10 minutes. Press Start/Pause to begin cooking. 6. Serve with creamed salad if desired. Bon appétit!

Salmon Cakes

Prep Time: 15 minutes | Cook Time: 13 minutes | Servings: 4

½ teaspoon chipotle powder

½ teaspoon butter, at room temperature

⅓ teaspoon smoked cayenne pepper

½ teaspoon dried parsley flakes

⅓ teaspoon ground black pepper

1-pound salmon, chopped into ½ inch pieces

1½ tablespoons milk

½ white onion, peeled and finely chopped

1 teaspoon fine sea salt

2 tablespoons coconut flour

2 tablespoons parmesan cheese, grated

¼ cup seasoned breadcrumbs

1. In a large mixing bowl, combine all ingredients except the breadcrumbs. 2. Shape the mixture into cakes and roll each cake over the seasoned breadcrumbs. Then, refrigerate for about 2 hours. 3. Place the fish cakes in the Crisper Tray. Slide the Crisper Tray into shelf position 4/5. Select the Airfry setting. Set the temperature to 395°F and the time to 13 minutes. Press Start/Pause to begin cooking. Flip them halfway through the cooking time. 4. Drizzle a dollop of sour cream before serving if desired. Enjoy!

Lemon-Butter Sea Scallops

Prep Time: 15 minutes | Cook Time: 15 minutes | Servings: 4

1-pound large sea scallops

Sea salt

Freshly ground black pepper

Avocado oil spray

¼ cup (4 tablespoons) unsalted butter

1 tablespoon freshly squeezed lemon juice

1 teaspoon minced garlic

¼ teaspoon red pepper flakes

1. Pat dry the scallops with a paper towel. 2. Season the scallops with salt and black pepper, then place them on a plate and refrigerate for 15 minutes. 3. Spray the crisper tray with oil, and place the scallops in a single layer. Spray the top of the scallops with oil spray. 4. Slide the Crisper Tray into shelf position 4/5. Select the Airfry setting. Set the temperature to 350°F and the time to 12 minutes. Press Start/Pause to begin cooking. Flip them halfway through the cooking time. 5. Meanwhile, combine the butter, garlic, lemon juice, and red pepper flakes in a small ramekin. 6. Remove the cooked scallops from the air fryer. Place the ramekin in the air fryer and cook for about 3 minutes until the butter melts. Stir. 7. Toss the scallops with the warm butter and serve.

Swordfish and Cherry Tomato Skewers

Prep Time: 40 minutes | Cook Time: 8 minutes | Servings: 4

1 pound filleted swordfish

¼ cup avocado oil

2 tablespoons freshly squeezed lemon juice

1 tablespoon minced fresh parsley

2 teaspoons Dijon mustard

Sea salt

Freshly ground black pepper

3 ounces cherry tomatoes

1. Cut fish into 1½-inch chunks; discard any bones. 2. In a big bowl, whisk together the oil, parsley, lemon juice and Dijon mustard. Season with salt and pepper. Add fish pieces and toss to coat. Cover and marinate the fish in the refrigerator for 30 minutes. 3. Remove fish from marinade. Thread fish and cherry tomatoes onto 4 skewers alternately. 4. Place the skewers in the Crisper Tray. Slide the Crisper Tray into shelf position 4/5. Select the Airfry setting. Set the temperature to 400°F and the time to 3 minutes. 5. Flip the skewers and cook for an additional 3 to 5 minutes, until the fish is cooked through and an instant-read thermometer reads 140°F.

Blackened Red Snapper

Prep Time: 10 minutes | Cook Time: 10 minutes | Servings: 4

1½ teaspoons black pepper

¼ teaspoon thyme

¼ teaspoon garlic powder

⅛ teaspoon cayenne pepper

1 teaspoon olive oil

4 4-ounce red snapper fillet portions, skin on

4 thin slices lemon

Cooking spray

1. In a small bowl, mix up the spices and oil. Rub this mixture on both sides of the fish. 2. Spray the baking pan with nonstick cooking spray and lay the snapper steaks inside, skin-side down. Top on each piece of fish with a lemon slice. 3. Slide the baking pan into shelf position 2. Select the Fish setting. Set the temperature to 390°F and the time to 10 minutes. Press Start/Pause to begin cooking. Flip them halfway through the cooking time. Serve warm.

Savory Crab Cakes

Prep Time: 25 minutes | Cook Time: 14 minutes | Servings: 4

Avocado oil spray

⅓ cup red onion, diced

¼ cup red bell pepper, diced

8 ounces lump crabmeat, picked over for shells

3 tablespoons finely ground blanched almond flour

1 large egg, beaten

1 tablespoon sugar-free mayonnaise (homemade, here, or store-bought)

2 teaspoons Dijon mustard

⅛ teaspoon cayenne pepper

Sea salt

Freshly ground black pepper

Elevated Tartar Sauce, for serving

Lemon wedges, for serving

1. Spray the baking pan with oil spray. Place the onion and red bell pepper in the pan and spray them with oil. Slide the baking pan into shelf position 4/5. Select the Vegetables setting. Set the temperature to 400°F and the time to 7 minutes. Press Start/Pause to begin cooking. Cook until tender. 2. Transfer the vegetables to a large bowl and add the crabmeat, egg, almond flour, mustard, mayonnaise, and cayenne pepper. Season with salt and black pepper. Stir until well combined. 3. Using your hands, form the mixture into four 1-inch-thick cakes. Cover with plastic wrap and refrigerate for 1 hour. 4. Place the crab cakes in a single layer in the crisper tray and spray them with oil. 5. Air fry at 400°F for 4 minutes. Flip the crab cakes and spray with more oil. Cook for 3 minutes more, until the internal temperature of the crab cakes reaches 155°F. 6. Squeeze with fresh lemon juice and serve with tartar sauce.

Coconut Shrimp

Prep Time: 15 minutes | Cook Time: 17 minutes | Servings: 4

¾ cup unsweetened shredded coconut

¾ cup coconut flour

1 teaspoon garlic powder

¼ teaspoon cayenne pepper

Sea salt

Freshly ground black pepper

2 large eggs

1 pound fresh extra-large or jumbo shrimp, peeled and deveined

Avocado oil spray

1. In a medium bowl, combine the coconut flour, shredded coconut, garlic powder, and cayenne pepper. Season with salt and black pepper. 2. Beat the eggs in a small bowl. 3. Pat dry the shrimp with paper towels. Dip each shrimp in the eggs and then roll in the coconut mixture. Gently press the coating onto the shrimp to help it adhere. 4. Place the coated shrimp in a single layer in the crisper tray and spray with oil. 5. Slide the Crisper Tray into shelf position 4/5. Select the Airfry setting. Set the temperature to 400°F and the time to 9 minutes. Press Start/Pause to begin cooking. 6. Then flip and spray them with more oil. Cook for an additional 8 minutes, until the center of the shrimp is opaque and cooked through.

Delicious Seafood Patties

Prep Time: 10 minutes | Cook Time: 12 minutes | Servings: 4

8 ounces imitation crabmeat

4 ounces leftover cooked fish (such as cod, pollock, or haddock)

2 tablespoons minced green onion

2 tablespoons minced celery

¾ cup crushed saltine cracker crumbs

2 tablespoons light mayonnaise

1 teaspoon prepared yellow mustard

1 tablespoon Worcestershire sauce, plus 2 teaspoons

2 teaspoons dried parsley flakes

½ teaspoon dried dill weed, crushed

½ teaspoon garlic powder

½ teaspoon Old Bay Seasoning

½ cup panko breadcrumbs

Oil for misting or cooking spray

1. Finely shred crabmeat and fish with knives or a food processor. 2. In a large bowl, mix together all ingredients except panko and oil. 3. Shape the mixture into 8 small, fat patties. 4. Roll each patty in panko crumbs to coat well. Spray both sides of the patties with oil or cooking spray. 5. Arrange the patties in the crisper tray. Slide the Crisper Tray into shelf position 4/5. Select the Airfry setting. Set the temperature to 390°F and the time to 12 minutes. Press Start/Pause to begin cooking. Flip them halfway through the cooking

Spicy Shrimp with Garlic Butter

Prep Time: 10 minutes | Cook Time: 10 minutes | Servings: 4

1 pound fresh large shrimp, peeled and deveined

1 tablespoon avocado oil

2 teaspoons minced garlic, divided

½ teaspoon red pepper flakes

Sea salt

Freshly ground black pepper

2 tablespoons unsalted butter, melted

2 tablespoons chopped fresh parsley

1. In a large bowl, too the shrimp with avocado oil, red pepper flakes and 1 teaspoon of minced garlic. Season with salt and black pepper. 2. Arrange the shrimp in a single layer in the crisper tray. Work in batches if necessary. Air fry at 350°F for 6 minutes. Flip the shrimp and cook for 2 to 4 minutes longer, until their internal temperature reaches 120°F. 3. Meanwhile, in a small saucepan over medium heat, melt the butter and stir in the remaining garlic. 4. Transfer the cooked shrimp to a bowl, add the garlic butter and stir well. Top with the parsley and serve warm.

Almond-Crusted Fish Fillets

Prep Time: 15 minutes | Cook Time: 10 minutes | Servings: 4

4 4-ounce fish fillets

¾ cup breadcrumbs

¼ cup sliced almonds, crushed

2 tablespoons lemon juice

⅛ teaspoon cayenne

salt and pepper

¾ cup flour

1 egg, beaten with 1 tablespoon water

Oil for misting or cooking spray

1. Slice the fillet lengthwise down the middle and cut into 8 pieces. 2. In a shallow bowl, combine the breadcrumbs and almonds. 3. In a small bowl, mix up the lemon juice and cayenne. Rub the mixture on all sides of fish. 4. Season the fish with salt and black pepper. 5. Place the flour on a sheet of wax paper. 6. Roll fillets in the flour, then dip in the egg wash, and finally roll in the crumb mixture. 7. Spray both sides of fish with oil or cooking spray. 8. Spray the baking pan with oil and lay fillets inside. 9. Slide the baking pan into shelf position 2. Select the Fish setting. Set the temperature to 390°F and the time to 10 minutes. Press Start/Pause to begin cooking. Flip them halfway through the cooking time.

Coconut-Shrimp Po' Boys

Prep Time: 20 minutes | Cook Time: 7 minutes | Servings: 4

½ cup cornstarch

2 eggs

2 tablespoons milk

¾ cup shredded coconut

½ cup panko breadcrumbs

1 pound (31–35 count) shrimp, peeled and deveined

Old Bay Seasoning

Oil for misting or cooking spray

2 large hoagie rolls

Honey mustard or light mayonnaise

1½ cups shredded lettuce

1 large tomato, thinly sliced

1. Place cornstarch in a shallow bowl. 2. In another shallow bowl, whisk together eggs and milk. 3. In a third bowl, combine the coconut and panko crumbs. 4. Sprinkle the shrimp with Old Bay Seasoning. 5. Coat the shrimp in cornstarch, then dip in the egg mixture and shake off any excess, and finally roll in coconut mixture to coat well. 6. Spray both sides of the coated shrimp with oil and arrange them in a single layer in the crisper tray. 7. Air fry at 390°F for 5 minutes.

To Assemble:

1. Cut each hoagie lengthwise, leaving one long edge intact. 2. Bake at 390°F for 1 to 2 minutes until heated through. 3. Remove the buns; break apart and place them on 4 plates, cut side up. 4. Spread the honey mustard and/or mayonnaise on top. 5. Then top with the shredded lettuce, tomato slices, and coconut shrimp.

Catfish Nuggets

Prep Time: 10 minutes | Cook Time: minutes | Servings: 4

2 medium catfish fillets, cut in chunks (approximately 1 x 2 inch)

Salt and pepper

2 eggs

2 tablespoons skim milk

½ cup cornstarch

1 cup panko breadcrumbs, crushed

Oil for misting or cooking spray

1. Season the catfish chunks with salt and black pepper. 2. In a small bowl, whisk together the eggs and milk. 3. Place the cornstarch in a second bowl. 4. Place the breadcrumbs in a third bowl. 5. Coat catfish chunks in cornstarch, then dip in egg wash and shake off any excess, finally roll in the breadcrumbs. 6. Spray all sides of the catfish chunks with oil or cooking spray. 7. Place chunks in the baking pan in a single layer, leaving space between each. 8. Slide the baking pan into shelf position 2. Select the Fish setting. Set the temperature to 390°F and the time to 8 minutes. Press Start/Pause to begin cooking. Flip them halfway through the cooking time. Serve warm.

Shrimp Caesar Salad

Prep Time: 25 minutes | Cook Time: 5 minutes | Servings: 4

12 ounces fresh large shrimp, peeled and deveined

1 tablespoon plus 1 teaspoon freshly squeezed lemon juice, divided

4 tablespoons olive oil or avocado oil, divided

2 garlic cloves, minced, divided

¼ teaspoon sea salt, plus additional to season the marinade

¼ teaspoon freshly ground black pepper, plus more to season the marinade

⅓ cup sugar-free mayonnaise (homemade, here, or store-bought)

2 tablespoons freshly grated Parmesan cheese

1 teaspoon Dijon mustard

1 tinned anchovy, mashed

12 ounces romaine hearts, torn

1. Place the shrimp in a large bowl and toss with 1 tablespoon of olive oil, 1 tablespoon of lemon juice, and 1 minced garlic clove. Season with salt and black pepper. Refrigerate for 15 minutes. 2. In a blender, combine the Parmesan cheese, mayonnaise, Dijon mustard, the remaining minced garlic clove, the remaining lemon juice, anchovy, ¼ teaspoon of salt, and ¼ teaspoon of pepper. Process the mixture until smooth. With blender running, slowly add remaining 3 tablespoons oil. Pour mixture into a jar, seal and refrigerate until ready to use. 3. Remove the shrimp from the marinade and place it in the crisper tray in a single layer. Slide the Crisper Tray into shelf position 4/5. Select the Airfry setting. Set the temperature to 400°F and the time to 2 minutes. Press Start/Pause to begin cooking. Flip the shrimp and cook for an additional 2 to 4 minutes, or until the flesh turns opaque. 4. Place the romaine hearts in a large bowl and toss with the desired amount of dressing. Top with the shrimp and serve immediately.

Chapter 6 Snacks and Appetizers

Crispy Rice Logs

Prep Time: 25 minutes | Cook Time: 5 minutes | Yields: 8 rice logs

1½ cups cooked jasmine or sushi rice

¼ teaspoon salt

2 teaspoons five-spice powder

2 teaspoons diced shallots

1 tablespoon tamari sauce

1 egg, beaten

1 teaspoon sesame oil

2 teaspoons water

⅓ cup plain breadcrumbs

¾ cup panko breadcrumbs

2 tablespoons sesame seeds

Orange Marmalade Dipping Sauce:

½ cup all-natural orange marmalade

1 tablespoon soy sauce

1. Make the rice per the package instructions. Meanwhile, prepare the dipping sauce by mixing the marmalade and soy sauce; set aside. 2. In a bowl, mix together the cooked rice, five-spice powder, salt, shallots, and tamari sauce. 3. Divide the rice into 8 equal pieces. Mold each piece into a log shape with your slightly damp hands. Chill in the refrigerator for 10 to 15 minutes. 4. In a shallow bowl, whisk together the egg, sesame oil, and water. 5. Place the plain breadcrumbs on a sheet of wax paper. 6. Combine the panko breadcrumbs with the sesame seeds; place on another sheet of wax paper. 7. Roll the rice logs in the plain breadcrumbs, and then dip in the egg wash, finally dip in the panko and sesame seeds. 8. Air fry the logs at 390°F for about 5 minutes, until golden brown. 9. Let Cool slightly and serve with the orange marmalade dipping sauce.

Buttered Cheese Apple Rollups

Prep Time: 10 minutes | Cook Time: 5 minutes | Servings: 8

8 slices whole wheat sandwich bread

4 ounces Colby Jack cheese, grated

½ small apple, chopped

2 tablespoons butter, melted

1. Remove the crusts and flatten the bread slices with a rolling pin. Press hard so the bread will be thin. 2. Top the bread slices with cheese and chopped apples, dividing the ingredients evenly. 3. Roll each slice of bread tightly and secure with one or two toothpicks. 4. Place the rolls in the baking pan and brush outside of the rolls with melted butter. 5. Slide the baking pan into shelf position 4/5. Select the Bake setting. Set the temperature to 390°F and the time to 5 minutes. Press Start/Pause to begin cooking. Bake until outside is crisp and nicely browned.

Bacon Wrapped Onion Rings

Prep Time: 10 minutes | Cook Time: 15 minutes | Servings: 2

1 onion, cut into ½-inch slices

1 teaspoon curry powder

1 teaspoon cayenne pepper

Salt and ground black pepper, to your

liking

8 strips bacon

¼ cup spicy ketchup

1. Fill a bowl with cold water and place the onion rings inside. Allow them to soak about 20 minutes. Then drain the onion rings and pat them dry using a kitchen towel. 2. Sprinkle curry powder, salt, cayenne pepper, and black pepper over the onion rings. 3. Wrap one layer of bacon around each onion ring, trimming any excess. Secure the rings with toothpicks. 4. Spray the crisper tray with cooking spray and place the wrapped onion rings inside. 5. Slide the Crisper Tray into shelf position 4/5. Select the Airfry setting. Set the temperature to 360°F and the time to 15 minutes. Press Start/Pause to begin cooking. Flip them halfway through the cooking time. 6. Serve with spicy ketchup. Bon appétit!

Cauliflower Popcorn

Prep Time: 10 minutes | Cook Time: 11 minutes | Servings: 4

1 cup cauliflower florets

1 teaspoon ground turmeric

2 eggs, beaten

2 tablespoons almond flour

1 teaspoon salt

Cooking spray

1. Cut the cauliflower into small pieces and sprinkle with turmeric and salt. Then dip the vegetables into the eggs and coat with almond flour. 2. Place the cauliflower popcorn in the Crisper Tray in one layer. Slide the Crisper Tray into shelf position 4/5. Select the Airfry setting. Set the temperature to 400°F and the time to 7 minutes. Press Start/Pause to begin cooking. Flip them halfway through the cooking time. 3. Shake well and cook them for an additional 4 minutes.

Yummy Parmesan Pecan Balls

Prep Time: 10 minutes | Cook Time: 8 minutes | Servings: 6

4 pecans, grinded

3 tablespoons dried parsley

1 teaspoon onion powder

1 egg, beaten

2 oz. Parmesan, grated

1. In a bowl, combine the pecans with dried basil, egg, onion powder, and Parmesan. Stir to mix well. 2. Make the mixture into small balls and place them in the crisper tray. 3. Air fry them at 375°F for 4 minutes per side.

Five-Spiced Chicken Wings

Prep Time: 10 minutes | Cook Time: 14 minutes | Servings: 8

2 pounds chicken wings

½ cup Asian-style salad dressing

2 tablespoons Chinese five-spice powder

1. Cut off chicken wing tips and discard or freeze for soup. Cut the remaining chicken wing pieces in half at the joint. 2. Place chicken wing pieces in a large sealable plastic bag. Pour in the Asian-style dressing, seal the bag, and spread the marinade over the chicken wings. Refrigerate for at least one hour. 3. Remove the chicken wings from bag, drain excess marinade. Place wings in the crisper tray and slide the Baking Pan into shelf position 6 to catch the drippings. 4. Select the Wings setting. Set the temperature to 360°F and the time to 14 minutes. Press Start/Pause to begin cooking. Flip them halfway through the cooking time. 5. Transfer the cooked chicken wings to plate in a single layer. Sprinkle half of the Chinese five-spice powder on the chicken wings. Flip them over and sprinkle other side with remaining seasoning.

Radish Chips

Prep Time: 5 minutes | Cook Time: 15 minutes | Servings: 4

16 ounces radishes, thinly sliced

A pinch of salt and black pepper

2 tablespoons coconut oil, melted

1. In a bowl, toss the radish slices with salt, black pepper and the oil. 2. Place them in the crisper tray and air fry at 400°F for 15 minutes, flipping them halfway through. Serve as a snack.

Ranch Cashew Bowls

Prep Time: 5 minutes | Cook Time: 5 minutes | Servings: 4

4 oz. cashew

1 teaspoon ranch seasoning

1 teaspoon sesame oil

1. In a bowl, toss the cashew with ranch seasoning and sesame oil and place in the baking pan. 2. Bake at 375°F for 4 minutes. Then shake them well and cook for 1 more minute.

Herbed Olive Dip

Prep Time: 5 minutes | Cook Time: 5 minutes | Servings: 6

1 cup black olives, pitted and chopped

¼ cup capers

½ cup olive oil

3 tablespoons lemon juice

2 garlic cloves, minced

2 teaspoon apple cider vinegar

1 cup parsley leaves

1 cup basil leaves

A pinch of salt and black pepper

1. Combine all the ingredients in a blender. Pulse well and transfer the mixture to a ramekin. 2. Slide the wire rack into shelf position 4/5. Place the ramekin on the wire rack. Select the Airfry setting. Set the temperature to 350°F and the time to 5 minutes. Press Start/Pause to begin cooking. 3. Serve as a snack.

Bacon-Wrapped Chicken

Prep Time: 10 minutes | Cook Time: 10 minutes | Servings: 2

6 oz. chicken fillet

2 oz. bacon, sliced

1 teaspoon avocado oil

¼ teaspoon ground black pepper

1. Cut the chicken into chunks and wrap them in bacon. Then slice the wrapped chicken bites and sprinkle with black pepper and avocado oil. 2. Arrange them in the Crisper Tray. Slide the Crisper Tray into shelf position 4/5. Select the Airfry setting. Set the temperature to 400°F and the time to 10 minutes. Press Start/Pause to begin cooking. Flip them halfway through the cooking time.

Spinach Pie

Prep Time: 15 minutes | Cook Time: 15 minutes | Servings: 6

½ cup almond flour

6 eggs

2 cup spinach, chopped

1 oz. scallions, chopped

1 teaspoon sesame oil

1 tablespoon cream cheese

½ teaspoon baking powder

1 tablespoon butter, softened

1 teaspoon ground black pepper

1. In a mixing bowl, combine the almond flour, baking powder and butter. Then beat in 2 eggs and mix gently. After that, knead the dough until it does not stick to your hands. Place the dough in the baking pan and flatten it to get the shape of the pie crust. 2. Select the Pastry setting. Set the temperature to 365°F and the time to 10 minutes. When the appliance has preheated, slide the baking pan into shelf position 4/5. Press Start/Pause to begin cooking. Cook until the bread is golden. 3. Meanwhile, in a skillet over medium heat, warm the sesame oil. Add scallions and cook them for 2 minutes. 4. Then add the vegetables and add chopped spinach and cream cheese. Stir and cook the greens for 5 minutes. Sprinkle with ground black pepper and place the spinach mixture in the pie crust and flatten gently. 5. Bake the pie at 365°F for 5 minutes.

Nutty Chicken, Berries and Spinach Bowls

Prep Time: 10 minutes | Cook Time: 25 minutes | Servings: 2

1 chicken breast, skinless, boneless and cut into strips

2 cups baby spinach

1 cup blueberries

6 strawberries, chopped

½ cup walnuts, chopped

3 tablespoons balsamic vinegar

1 tablespoon olive oil

3 tablespoons feta cheese, crumbled

1. Heat oil in a pan suitable for an air fryer over medium heat; add meat and sauté for 5 minutes. Add remaining ingredients except spinach; toss well. 2. Slide the wire rack into shelf position 4/5. Place the pan on the wire rack. Select the Airfry setting. Set the temperature to 370°F and the time to 15 minutes. Press Start/Pause to begin cooking. 3. When cooking time is up, add the spinach and toss well; cook for 5 minutes more, divide into bowls and serve.

Zucchini and Tomato Salsa

Prep Time: 5 minutes | Cook Time: 15 minutes | Servings: 6

1 and ½ pounds zucchinis, roughly cubed

2 spring onions, chopped

2 tomatoes, cubed

Salt and black pepper to the taste

1 tablespoon balsamic vinegar

1. Combine all the ingredients in the baking pan and toss well. 2. Slide the pan into shelf position 4/5. Select the Vegetables setting. Set the temperature to 360°F and the time to 15 minutes. Press Start/Pause to begin cooking. 3. Divide the salsa into cups and serve cold.

Basil Salmon Bites

Prep Time: 5 minutes | Cook Time: 10 minutes | Servings: 6

1-pound salmon fillet, roughly chopped

1 tablespoon avocado oil

1 teaspoon dried basil

1 teaspoon ground black pepper

1. Toss the chopped salmon with dried basil and black pepper. 2. Place the fish pieces in the crisper tray and sprinkle with avocado oil. 3. Air fry the salmon bites at 375°F for 10 minutes.

Eggplant Slices

Prep Time: 10 minutes | Cook Time: 25 minutes | Servings: 4

1 eggplant, sliced

½ teaspoon salt

1 teaspoon nutritional yeast

1. Sprinkle the eggplant slices with salt and nutritional yeast. 2. Place them in the crisper tray. Slide the Crisper Tray into shelf position 4/5. Select the Vegetables setting. Set the temperature to 360°F and the time to 25 minutes. Press Start/Pause to begin cooking. Flip them halfway through the cooking time.

Spiced Pork Sticks

Prep Time: 10 minutes | Cook Time: 12 minutes | Servings: 4

2 eggs, beaten

4 tablespoons flax meal

½ teaspoon chili powder

¼ teaspoon ground cumin

8 oz. pork loin

1 teaspoon sunflower oil

1. Cut the pork loin into the sticks. Sprinkle them with chili powder and cumin powder. Dip the pork sticks in the eggs and coat in the flax meal. 2. Place the pork sticks in the crisper tray and sprinkle with sunflower oil. 3. Slide the Crisper Tray into shelf position 4/5. Select the Airfry setting. Set the temperature to 400°F and the time to 12 minutes. Press Start/Pause to begin cooking. Flip them halfway through the cooking time.

Italian Popcorn Chicken

Prep Time: 10 minutes | Cook Time: 12 minutes | Servings: 6

2 cups ground chicken

1 teaspoon Italian seasonings

1 egg, beaten

¼ cup coconut flour

1 tablespoon avocado oil

1. In a bowl, mix the ground chicken with egg, Italian seasonings and coconut flour. 2. Make the small popcorn-shaped balls from the chicken mixture and place in the crisper tray in one layer. 3. Sprinkle the popcorn balls with avocado oil. Air fry at 365°F for 6 minutes on each side.

Mini Chicken Wontons

Prep Time: 15 minutes | Cook Time: 10 minutes | Servings: 6

1-pound chicken fillet, boiled

1 tablespoon cream cheese

1 teaspoon chili powder

1 teaspoon garlic powder

6 wonton wraps

1 egg, beaten

1 tablespoon avocado oil

1. Shred the chicken and mix it with egg, cream cheese, garlic powder and chili powder. 2. Then place the chicken mixture on the wonton wraps and roll them up. 3. Place the mini chicken wontons in the crisper tray. 4. Sprinkle avocado oil over the chicken pies and slide the Crisper Tray into shelf position 4/5. Select the Airfry setting. Set the temperature to 375°F and the time to 10 minutes. Press Start/Pause to begin cooking.

Aromatic Brussels Sprout

Prep Time: 10 minutes | Cook Time: 15 minutes | Servings: 4

1 pound Brussels sprouts, ends and yellow leaves removed and halved lengthwise

Salt and black pepper, to taste

1 tablespoon toasted sesame oil

1 teaspoon fennel seeds

Chopped fresh parsley, for garnish

1. In a resealable plastic bag, combine the Brussels sprouts, sesame oil, salt, pepper, and fennel seeds. Seal the bag and shake to coat well. 2. Place the seasoned Brussels sprouts in the crisper tray. Slide the Crisper Tray into shelf position 4/5. Select the Vegetables setting. Set the temperature to 380°F and the time to 15 minutes. Press Start/Pause to begin cooking. Flip them halfway through the cooking time. 3. Sprinkle with fresh parsley and serve hot!

Balsamic Tomato Mozzarella Salad

Prep Time: 5 minutes | Cook Time: 12 minutes | Servings: 6

1 pound tomatoes, sliced

1 tablespoon balsamic vinegar

1 tablespoon ginger, grated

½ teaspoon coriander, ground

1 teaspoon sweet paprika

1 teaspoon chili powder

1 cup mozzarella, shredded

1. Combine all the ingredients except the mozzarella in a pan that fits your air fryer, toss well. 2. Slide the wire rack into shelf position 4/5. Place the pan on the wire rack. Select the Airfry setting. Set the temperature to 360°F and the time to 12 minutes. Press Start/Pause to begin cooking. 3. Divide into bowls and sprinkle with mozzarella. Serve cold as an appetizer.

Chapter 7 Dessert and Drinks

Soft Blackberry Almond Cake

Prep Time: 10 minutes | Cook Time: 25 minutes | Servings: 4

2 eggs, whisked

4 tablespoons swerve

2 tablespoons ghee, melted

¼ cup almond milk

1 and ½ cups almond flour

1 cup blackberries, chopped

½ teaspoon baking powder

1 teaspoon lemon zest, grated

1 teaspoon lemon juice

1. Combine all the ingredients in a bowl and whisk well. Line a cake pan that fits the air fryer lined with parchment paper and pour this batter into the pan. 2. Slide the wire rack into shelf position 4/5. Place the cake pan on the wire rack. Select the Bake setting. Set the temperature to 340°F and the time to 25 minutes. Press Start/Pause to begin cooking. 3. Cool the cake down, slice and serve.

Apple Pies

Prep Time: 20 minutes | Cook Time: 15 minutes | Servings: 4

1 refrigerated piecrust (store-bought or see below)

1 pound McIntosh apples

2 tablespoons packed brown sugar

2 tablespoons dried cranberries

2 teaspoons all-purpose flour

½ teaspoon ground cinnamon

⅛ teaspoon grated nutmeg

¼ teaspoon grated orange rind

Pinch salt

1. Roll the piecrust out on a floured surface. Cut out three (4½-inch) rounds using a glass and place on a baking sheet to chill. 2. Peel, core, and cut the apples into half-slices. In a microwave-safe bowl, toss the apples with cranberries, brown sugar, flour, orange rind, cinnamon, nutmeg, and a pinch of salt. Microwave on High heat for about 2½ minutes or just until softened, stirring once. 3. Divide the filling among 3 ramekins or custard cups. Place the piecrust rounds on top, forming a fluted edge, and cut a slit in the center. 4. Slide the wire rack into shelf position 4/5. Place the ramekins on the wire rack. Select the Bake setting. Set the temperature to 350°F and the time to 12 minutes. Press Start/Pause to begin cooking. 5. Let them cool for 10 minutes and serve.

Goji Coffee Surprise with Flaxseed

Prep Time: 5 minutes | Cook Time: 0 minutes | Servings: 1

2 heaped tbsp flaxseed, ground

100ml cooking cream 35% fat

½ tsp cocoa powder, dark and

unsweetened

1 tbsp goji berries

Freshly brewed coffee

1. In a bowl, mix together the cream, flaxseeds, cocoa and coffee. 2. Season with goji berries. 3. Serve!

Homemade Coconut Cookies

Prep Time: 15 minutes | Cook Time: 10 minutes | Servings: 6

3 tablespoons coconut oil, softened

4 tablespoons coconut flour

2 tablespoons flax meal

2 tablespoons Monk fruit

1 teaspoon poppy seeds

½ teaspoon baking powder

½ teaspoon lemon juice

¼ teaspoon ground cardamom

Cooking spray

1. In a mixing bowl, combine the coconut flour, coconut oil, flax meal, ad Monk fruit. Then add the baking powder, poppy seeds, lemon juice, and cardamom. 2. Knead the mixture into soft but non-sticky dough with your fingertips. Then make the cookies from the dough. 3. Spray the baking pan with cooking spray. Place the cookies in the pan and bake them at 375°F for 10 minutes.

Cinnamon Plums

Prep Time: 5 minutes | Cook Time: 20 minutes | Servings: 4

2 teaspoons cinnamon powder

4 plums, halved

4 tablespoons butter, melted

3 tablespoons swerve

1. Combine the plums with the remaining ingredients in the baking pan and toss well. 2. Bake at 300°F for 20 minutes. Divide into cups and serve cold.

Chocolate Molten Cupcakes

Prep Time: 20 minutes | Cook Time: 15 minutes | Servings: 4

¼ cup butter (½ stick), cut into pieces, plus more for greasing the custard cups

2 tablespoons granulated sugar, plus more for dusting

2 ounces semisweet chocolate, chopped

2 tablespoons heavy or whipping cream

¼ teaspoon vanilla extract

2 tablespoons all-purpose flour

1 large egg

1 large egg yolk

Confectioners' sugar, for dusting

Whipped cream or ice cream, for serving (optional)

1. Grease four 6-ounce custard cups and dust with granulated sugar. 2. In a medium saucepan over low heat, add the butter, chocolate, and cream, stirring occasionally, until chocolate has melted and mixture is smooth. Remove the pan from heat. Add vanilla and whisk in flour until the mixture is smooth. 3. In a small bowl, using a whisk, beat 2 tablespoons granulated sugar, whole egg, and yolk on high speed until thick and pale yellow, about 5 minutes. Add the egg mixture, one third at a time, to the chocolate mixture until combined. 4. Divide the batter evenly among the prepared custard cups. Slide the wire rack into shelf position 4/5. Place the custard cups on the wire rack. Select the Bake setting. Set the temperature to 300°F and the time to 10 minutes. Press Start/Pause to begin cooking. Cook until firm at edges and soft in center when pressed lightly. 5. Let them cool on a wire rack for 5 minutes. Run a thin knife around the rim of the cup to loosen the cakes; invert onto plates and dust with confectioners' sugar. 6. Serve with whipped cream or ice cream to your liking.

Delicious Chocolate-Hazelnut Croissants

Prep Time: 10 minutes | Cook Time: 8 minutes | Servings: 4

1 sheet frozen puff pastry, thawed

⅓ cup chocolate-hazelnut spread

1 large egg, beaten

1. On a lightly floured countertop, roll out puff pastry to a 14-inch square. Cut pastry into quarters to form 4 squares. Then cut each square diagonally into 8 triangles. 2. Spread each triangle with 2 teaspoons chocolate hazelnut spread; roll up pastry, starting at wider end. Brush top of each roll with egg. 3. Arrange them in the baking pan. Bake at 375°F for 8 minutes until the pastry is golden brown. 4. Allow them to cool for a few minutes. Serve and enjoy.

Dried Tart Cherries-Pecan Stuffed Apples

Prep Time: 10 minutes | Cook Time: 25 minutes | Servings: 4

4 Gala or Empire apples (about 1¼ pounds)

¼ cup chopped pecans

⅓ cup dried tart cherries

1 tablespoon melted butter

3 tablespoons brown sugar

¼ teaspoon allspice

Pinch salt

Ice cream, for serving

1. Cut ½ inch from top of each apple, reserving tops. Use a melon baller to dig the core from the stem end, but do not break through the bottom. 2. In a bowl, combine the pecans, cherries, brown sugar, butter, allspice, and a pinch of salt. Stuff the mixture into the hollow centers of the apples. Cover with the apple tops. Place the stuffed apples in the baking pan. Bake at 350°F for 20 to 25 minutes, or just until tender. 3. Serve with ice cream.

Banana Bread Pudding

Prep Time: 15 minutes | Cook Time: 25 minutes | Servings: 4

½ cup brown sugar

3 eggs

¾ cup half and half

1 teaspoon pure vanilla extract

6 cups cubed Kings Hawaiian bread (½-inch cubes), ½ pound

2 bananas, sliced

1 cup caramel sauce, plus more for serving

1. In a large bowl, combine the eggs, brown sugar, half and half and vanilla extract; whisk until the sugar is dissolved and the mixture is smooth. Add the cubed bread and toss to coat well. Let the bread rest for 10 minutes to absorb the liquid. 2. In a separate bowl, combine banana slices and caramel sauce. 3. Place half of the bread cubes in the bottom of 4 (8 ounce) greased ramekins. Divide the caramel and bananas among the ramekins; spoon them on top of the bread cubes. Top with the rest of the bread cubes and wrap each ramekin with aluminum foil, tenting the foil at the top to leave some room for the bread to puff up during cooking. 4. Slide the wire rack into shelf position 4/5. Place the ramekins on the wire rack. Select the Bake setting. Set the temperature to 350°F and the time to 25 minutes. Press Start/Pause to begin cooking. 5. Allow the puddings to cool slightly and drizzle with additional caramel sauce. Serve and enjoy!

Fluffy Chocolate Soufflés

Prep Time: 25 minutes | Cook Time: 15 minutes | Servings: 2

Butter and sugar for greasing the ramekins

3 ounces semi-sweet chocolate, chopped

¼ cup unsalted butter

2 eggs, yolks and white separated

3 tablespoons sugar

2 tablespoons all-purpose flour

½ teaspoon pure vanilla extract

Powdered sugar, for dusting the finished soufflés

Heavy cream, for serving

1. Butter two 6-ounce ramekins, then coat them with sugar by swirling it around and discarding the excess. 2. Next, melt the chocolate and butter together in a microwave-safe bowl. In another bowl, beat the egg yolks vigorously. Add the sugar and vanilla extract and beat well again. Drizzle in the chocolate mixture and stir to mix well. Add in the flour, combining until there are no lumps. 3. In a separate bowl, whisk the egg whites to the soft peak stage (the whites will almost stand up on the end of the whisk). Gently fold the whipped egg whites into the chocolate mixture in small batches. 4. Carefully pour the batter into the buttered ramekins, leaving about ½-inch at the top. Slide the wire rack into shelf position 4/5. Place the ramekins on the wire rack. Select the Bake setting. Set the temperature to 330°F and the time to 14 minutes. Press Start/Pause to begin cooking. Bake until the soufflés have risen nicely and are brown on top. 5. Dust with powdered sugar and serve with heavy cream.

Raspberry Chocolate Pudding

Prep Time: 35 minutes | Cook Time: 0 minutes | Servings: 1

3 tbsp. chia seeds

½ cup unsweetened milk

1 scoop chocolate protein powder

¼ cup raspberries, fresh or frozen

1 tsp honey

1. In a medium bowl, combine together the milk, protein powder and chia seeds. 2. Allow it to rest for 5 minutes; then add the honey and stir well. 3. Refrigerate for 30 minutes. 4. Top with raspberries and serve!

Sweet Creamy Plum

Prep Time: 10 minutes | Cook Time: 20 minutes | Servings: 4

1 pound plums, pitted and chopped

¼ cup swerve

1 tablespoon lemon juice

1½ cups heavy cream

1. Combine all the ingredients in a bowl and whisk well. Divide this mixture into 4 ramekins. 2. Slide the wire rack into shelf position 4/5. Place the ramekins on the wire rack. Select the Bake setting. Set the temperature to 340°F and the time to 20 minutes. Press Start/Pause to begin cooking. Serve cold.

Cream Cheese Coconut Pound Cake

Prep Time: 25 minutes | Cook Time: 30 minutes | Servings: 4

2 teaspoons cream cheese

1 teaspoon Truvia

1 teaspoon vanilla extract

½ cup heavy cream

1 egg, beaten

1 teaspoon baking powder

1 teaspoon apple cider vinegar

1½ cup coconut flour

2 tablespoons butter, softened

Cooking spray

1. Pour heavy cream into a bowl. Add egg, vanilla extract, apple cider vinegar, baking powder, and butter. Stir until homogenous. 2. Add the coconut flour and whisk the liquid until smooth. 3. Spray the pound cake mold with cooking spray. Pour the cake batter into the mold. Flatten its surface with the spatula. 4. Slide the wire rack into shelf position 4/5. Place the cake mold on the wire rack. Select the Bake setting. Set the temperature to 365°F and the time to 30 minutes. Press Start/Pause to begin cooking. 5. Once done cooking, allow it to cool to the room temperature. 6. In the meantime, whisk together cream cheese and Truvia in a shallow bowl. Then spread the sweet cream cheese over the pound cake. Slice the dessert on the servings.

Chocolate Berries Coconut Milk

Prep Time: 5 minutes | Cook Time: 0 minutes | Servings: 4

1 can unsweetened coconut milk

Berries of choice

Dark chocolate

1. Refrigerate the coconut milk for 24 hours. 2. Remove it from refrigerator and whip for 2-3 minutes. 3. Add the berries and season with the chocolate shavings. Serve!

Granola Bark

1 large egg white

⅓ cup maple syrup

1 teaspoon vanilla extract

¼ cup olive oil

¼ teaspoon salt

1½ cups old-fashioned oats

½ cup roasted, salted almonds, coarsely

chopped

¼ cup sunflower seeds

¾ teaspoon ground cinnamon

¼ cup almond flour

Milk and fresh fruit (such as berries and peaches), for serving (optional)

1. In a small bowl, gently whisk egg whites with a fork; measure out 1 tablespoon of whisked egg whites and set aside. Discard remaining egg whites or reserve for another use. 2. Cut a piece of parchment paper and lay it on the bottom and halfway up the sides of the baking pan, pressing the parchment paper against the sides and bottom. 3. In a small bowl, mix up the olive oil, maple syrup, vanilla, salt, and 1 tablespoon beaten egg white. In a large bowl, combine the oats, almond flour, almonds, sunflower seeds, and cinnamon. Add the wet mixture to the dry ingredients and mix thoroughly. 4. Press half the mixture into the prepared baking pan with the back of a spoon or wet hands. 5. Slide the baking pan into shelf position 4/5. Select the Bake setting. Set the temperature to 325°F and the time to 14 minutes. Press Start/Pause to begin cooking. Bake until golden brown all over. Do not stir. 6. Carefully remove granola from air fryer, grasping parchment paper on both sides; let it cool on parchment paper on wire rack for 1 hour before breaking into small pieces. Repeat with remaining oat mixture. 7. Serve with milk and fruit as needed. Store in an airtight container at room temperature for 1 week.

Raspberry Cheesecake

8 oz. cream cheese, softened

2 oz. heavy cream

½ tsp Splenda

1 tsp raspberries

1 tbsp Da Vinci Sugar-Free syrup, white chocolate flavor

1. Whisk all ingredients to a thick consistency. 2. Divide in cups. 3. Refrigerate for 30 minutes and serve.

Puff Pastry Apples

Prep Time: 30 minutes | Cook Time: 10 minutes | Servings: 4

3 Rome or Gala apples, peeled, cored

2 tablespoons sugar

1 teaspoon all-purpose flour

1 teaspoon ground cinnamon

⅛ teaspoon ground ginger

Pinch ground nutmeg

1 sheet puff pastry

1 tablespoon butter, cut into 4 pieces

1 egg, beaten

Vegetable oil

Vanilla ice cream (optional)

Caramel sauce (optional)

1. Cut the apple into thin half-moon slices, about ¼-inch thick. In a large bowl, combine the flour, ginger, sugar, cinnamon, and nutmeg. Add the apples to the bowl and toss gently until the apples are evenly coated with the spice mixture. Set aside. 2. Cut the puff pastry into 12-inch by 12-inch squares. Then cut the puff pastry into four 6-inch squares. Reserve the remaining puff pastry for decorating the apples at the end. 3. Divide the spiced apples among the four squares of puff pastry, stack the apples in the center of each square, and place them flat together in a circle. Place a piece of butter on top of the apples. 4. Brush the four edges of the puff pastry with egg wash. Bring the four corners of the pastry together to enclose the apple slices and pinch at the top to make a "beggar's purse" appetizer style. Fold the ends of the corners of the pastry down over the apples to make them look like leaves. Brush the entire apple with egg wash. 5. Use the remaining dough to make leaves to decorate the apples. Cut out 8 leaf shapes about 1½ inches long and use a paring knife to "draw" leaf veins on the pastry blades. 6. Place two leaves on top of each apple and tuck the ends of the leaves under the pastry in the center of the apple. Brush the tops of the leaves with more egg wash. Sprinkle some granulated sugar over the entire apple. 7. Spray the baking pan with oil. Place the apples in the pan and bake at 350°F for 6 minutes. Carefully turn the apples over and bake for another 4 minutes. 8. Serve warm with vanilla ice cream and drizzle with some caramel sauce.

Apple Crumble

Prep Time: 20 minutes | Cook Time: 50 minutes | Servings: 6

4 apples, peeled and thinly sliced

2 tablespoons sugar

1 tablespoon flour

1 teaspoon ground cinnamon

¼ teaspoon ground allspice

healthy pinch ground nutmeg

10 caramel squares, cut into small pieces

Crumble Topping:

¾ cup rolled oats

¼ cup sugar

⅓ cup flour

¼ teaspoon ground cinnamon

6 tablespoons butter, melted

1. In a large bowl, Combine the apples, flour, sugar, and spices and toss to coat well. Stir in the caramel pieces and mix well. Pour the apple mixture into a round baking pan that can fit in your air fryer. 2. To prepare the crumble topping, combine the flour, rolled oats, sugar and cinnamon in a small bowl. Add the melted butter and stir to mix well. Spread the crumble mixture over the apples. Cover the entire baking pan with aluminum foil. 3. Slide the wire rack into shelf position 4/5. Place the round baking pan on the wire rack. Select the Bake setting. Set the temperature to 330°F and the time to 25 minutes. Press Start/Pause to begin cooking. 4. Remove the aluminum foil and continue to bake for 25 minutes more. Serve warm with whipped cream or vanilla ice cream, if desired.

Conclusion

The Emeril Lagasse French Door Air Fryer Oven is a versatile kitchen tool, enabling you to air fry, bake, roast, and more. Its French door design adds elegance while saving space. Ideal for quick and efficient cooking, this oven delivers consistent, delicious results, whether for weeknight dinners or large gatherings. User-friendly controls and easy-to-clean components make it accessible to all, while included accessories like the Crisper Tray and Rotisserie Spit enhance its functionality. This appliance simplifies cooking, making it an essential addition to any kitchen, offering convenience, versatility, and healthier meal options.

The Emeril Lagasse French Door Air Fryer Oven Cookbook is your ultimate guide to mastering this versatile kitchen appliance. With carefully crafted recipes that showcase the full potential of the oven's multiple functions, this cookbook takes you on a culinary journey from simple weeknight meals to impressive dishes for special occasions. Each recipe is designed to help you create flavorful, healthy, and satisfying meals with ease. By integrating the Emeril Lagasse French Door Air Fryer Oven into your cooking routine, you'll discover how effortless and enjoyable meal preparation can be. Embrace the convenience, enhance your culinary skills, and delight in the delicious possibilities that this cookbook brings to your kitchen.

Appendix 1 Measurement Conversion Chart

VOLUME EQUIVALENTS (LIQUID)

US STANDARD	US STANDARD (OUNCES)	METRIC (APPROXIMATE)
2 tablespoons	1 fl.oz	30 mL
¼ cup	2 fl.oz	60 mL
½ cup	4 fl.oz	120 mL
1 cup	8 fl.oz	240 mL
1½ cup	12 fl.oz	355 mL
2 cups or 1 pint	16 fl.oz	475 mL
4 cups or 1 quart	32 fl.oz	1 L
1 gallon	128 fl.oz	4 L

VOLUME EQUIVALENTS (DRY)

US STANDARD	METRIC (APPROXIMATE)
⅛ teaspoon	0.5 mL
¼ teaspoon	1 mL
½ teaspoon	2 mL
¾ teaspoon	4 mL
1 teaspoon	5 mL
1 tablespoon	15 mL
¼ cup	59 mL
½ cup	118 mL
¾ cup	177 mL
1 cup	235 mL
2 cups	475 mL
3 cups	700 mL
4 cups	1 L

TEMPERATURES EQUIVALENTS

FAHRENHEIT (F)	CELSIUS (C) (APPROXIMATE)
225 °F	107 °C
250 °F	120 °C
275 °F	135 °C
300 °F	150 °C
325 °F	160 °C
350 °F	180 °C
375 °F	190 °C
400 °F	205 °C
425 °F	220 °C
450 °F	235 °C
475 °F	245 °C
500 °F	260 °C

WEIGHT EQUIVALENTS

US STANDARD	METRIC (APPROXINATE)
1 ounce	28 g
2 ounces	57 g
5 ounces	142 g
10 ounces	284 g
15 ounces	425 g
16 ounces (1 pound)	455 g
1.5 pounds	680 g
2 pounds	907 g

Appendix 2 Recipes Index

Made in United States
Orlando, FL
08 December 2024

55225112R00064